R VOICE,
INFLUENCE
IN THE WORLD

STEP
INTO
YOUR
Moxie

"As humorous as she is full of heart,
Alexia Vernon understands women's real and,
at times, self-imposed communication barriers.
Her recommendations are smart, practical, and, above all, fun."
— **BARBARA STANNY,** wealth coach and author of *Sacred Success*

ALEXIA VERNON

Praise for *Step into Your Moxie*

"Too many women still find it hard to speak up for themselves and t issues and causes they care about. *Step into Your Moxie* is a dynam much-needed guide for women who want to find their authentic voic sharpen their communication skills, and speak with passion and purpos in all areas of their lives." — **Claudia Chan,** author of *This Is How We Ris* and CEO of S.H.E. Summit

"In all the years I've been in my line of work as an author and speaker, there's been no one I'd rather get advice about 'voice' from than Alexia Vernon. Why? Because, as Alexia demonstrates in *Step into Your Moxie*, she understands everything that goes into being a powerful communicator and presenter, and she writes with memorable color and the utmost clarity." — **Alexandra Levit,** internationally bestselling author of *They Don't Teach Corporate in College* and *Humanity Works*

"Alexia Vernon is a firebrand. In *Step into Your Moxie*, she is so funny, professional, and self-effacing, it feels like a mastermind session, therapy, and a dinner date with your best friend all rolled into one. You can't teach people how to 'step into your moxie' if you're not doing it yourself with both hustle and heart, and as someone who has followed Alexia for years, I can say without a doubt that she is a true example of this for us all." — **Emily Bennington,** author of *Miracles at Work*

"We all have something to say, a part of us that is deeply real and powerful that's yearning to get out. But how do we share it with the world in a way that leaves us feeling seen, heard, understood, and embraced? *Step into Your Moxie* is the answer. Filled with compelling stories, raw honesty, and actionable ideas, Alexia Vernon's book gives readers permission to bring their full selves into everything they say." — **Jonathan Fields,** founder of Good Life Project and bestselling author of *How to Live a Good Life*

"Where passion, purpose, and skill collide, bliss resides. Alexia Vernon lives in this intersection, and her moxie is unmatched." — **Amy Jo Martin,** *New York Times* bestselling author of *Renegades Write the Rules* and host of the *Why Not Now?* podcast

"Alexia Vernon shares unflinchingly honest stories and advice from the front lines of life. Her decades of experience in speaking up, running a business, and coaching shine through and make this book a catalyst for readers to unleash more moxie in this world! Pick it up if you're ready (or want to be ready) to step into *your* spotlight."

— **Nathalie Lussier,** founder of AmbitionAlly.com

"*Step into Your Moxie* is a powerful read that reminds women to own their voice, recognize their worth, and speak with moxie. Alexia Vernon's work as a renowned speaking and leadership coach is apparent in this inspiring book. Her relatable and incredibly motivating advice is ideal for the business-driven, hardworking woman of today."

— **Emily Williams,** owner of I Heart My Life

"*Step into Your Moxie* is a must-read for any woman who wants to use her words to create meaningful impact. Alexia Vernon reveals how to confidently deliver vibrant, heartfelt, and authentic presentations and shares methods for using difficult conversations as tools for better communication. Her uncomplicated and straightforward techniques will help even the most reluctant speaker find her moxie."

— **Yvonne Tally,** author of *Breaking Up with Busy*

"I have had the opportunity to hear Alexia Vernon speak on women's leadership and have attended several of her trainings. Her mentoring has had a huge impact on many of the big speaking and thought-leadership breakthroughs I have had in the past few years. This book is like having a portable version of Alexia I can pop in my purse and take with me everywhere. " — **Gabriela Pereira,** author of *DIY MFA*

"If you've ever thought that leadership, speaking up and out, or stepping forward in your community or in your life was something 'other people' do, *Step into Your Moxie* is your guide to recognize why your voice matters and to help you step forward with more confidence. Alexia Vernon shows readers how to look at the discomfort that comes along with change, navigate conflict, and do the real work to emerge in their lives with more visibility and with authentic strength."

— **Kate Swoboda,** author of *The Courage Habit*

"This book delivers! Raw, transparent, and powerful, Alexia Vernon's *Step into Your Moxie* surprised and delighted me, but more than anything it forced to me think deeply and question my beliefs, behaviors, and attitudes about how I show up in the world. I learn best from examples and case studies, and they're perfectly sprinkled throughout the book to provide you with inspiration and clarity about developing your unique voice and moxie. Combine that with Alexia's templates, questions, exercises, and resources, and this is one book that you will refer to again and again."   — **Natalie Sisson,** author of *The Freedom Plan*

"In *Step into Your Moxie*, Alexia Vernon powerfully shows women how to speak up for themselves, step into the spotlight, and become the leaders they were born to be."

— **Selena Soo,** creator of Impacting Millions

"Alexia Vernon is the one to show you how to own your uniqueness and become the most compelling version of yourself."

— **Susie Moore,** founder of Five Minutes to Famous

"Alexia Vernon's powerful, thought-provoking stories and ideas will get you thinking, but more importantly, they will give you the tools and boost you need to *act* in powerful ways so you can step into your moxie."   — **Halelly Azulay,** leadership strategist and author of *Employee Development on a Shoestring*

"Alexia Vernon is a powerhouse. Her storytelling is masterful, her vulnerability absolute, and her insights brilliant. She had to lose her voice to help us find ours, but as you will see in *Step into Your Moxie*, it was well worth it."   — **Jodi Glickman,** author of *Great on the Job*

"If #MeToo has taught us anything, it is that powerful, brave, and truthful women are needed to topple tired and oppressive systems. *Step into Your Moxie* is the tool we have been waiting for to unlock female leadership so that our ideas, policies, products, and art take center stage. This book will give you the courage to show up, speak up, and claim your seat at the table."   — **Pamela Slim,** author of *Body of Work*

STEP
INTO
YOUR
Moxie

AMPLIFY YOUR VOICE, VISIBILITY, AND INFLUENCE IN THE WORLD

ALEXIA VERNON

New World Library
Novato, California

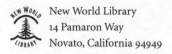

New World Library
14 Pamaron Way
Novato, California 94949

The material in this book is intended for education. No expressed or implied guarantee of the effects of using the recommendations can be given or liability taken. Some names and identifying characteristics have been changed to protect the privacy of others.

Text design by Tona Pearce Myers

Library of Congress Cataloging-in-Publication Data
Names: Vernon, Alexia, author.
Title: Step into your moxie : amplify your voice, visibility, and influence in the world / Alexia Vernon.
Description: Novato, California : New World Library, [2018] | Includes bibliographical references and index.
Identifiers: LCCN 2018022779 (print) | LCCN 2018036208 (ebook) | ISBN 9781608685592 (ebook) | ISBN 9781608685585 (alk. paper) | ISBN 9781608685592(eISBN)
Subjects: LCSH: Self-presentation. | Public speaking.
Classification: LCC BF697.5.S44 (ebook) | LCC BF697.5.S44 V47 2018 (print) | DDC 155.2--dc23
LC record available at https://lccn.loc.gov/2018022779

First printing, October 2018
ISBN 978-1-60868-558-5
Ebook ISBN 978-1-60868-559-2
Printed in Canada on 100% postconsumer-waste recycled paper

New World Library is proud to be a Gold Certified Environmentally Responsible Publisher. Publisher certification awarded by Green Press Initiative. www.greenpressinitiative.org

10   9   8   7   6   5   4   3   2   1

For my mom — thank you for giving me my words and the moxie to use them. I am who I am because of all the times you told me I was special (even when I felt anything but) and because of the support, space, and all-encompassing love you have given me since the moment I landed in your womb.

And for my dad — thank you for igniting my love of business and leadership and for encouraging all my dreams, especially the totally wackadoodle ones. I'm honored to be your Queen of the Fleet.

CONTENTS

Introduction   1

Chapter 1: Headgear, Hairy Legs,
and a Quarter Life of Humiliation   11

Chapter 2: Critics, Cops,
and Cheerleaders...Oh My!   25

Chapter 3: Bunnies Don't Belong Here
(but Cheetahs Do)   41

Chapter 4: Words, Words, Words   55

Chapter 5: Your Gut as Your Guide   71

Chapter 6: Declare Your Desired Destination   87

Chapter 7: Go for the Holy Yes   99

Chapter 8: Your Spotlight Is Waiting   117

Chapter 9: What to Say When
the Spotlight Is Yours   133

Chapter 10: Conflict Is the Pits, Until It Isn't   147

Chapter 11: Susan B. Anthony Didn't Fight
for Your Right to Be a Meanie   167

Chapter 12: When the Universe Bites Your Bum-Bum,
Don't Let Her Steal Your Voice   185

Chapter 13: Choose Legacy Over Fame   205

Acknowledgments   217

Notes   221

Index   227

About the Author   236

INTRODUCTION

About a decade ago it occurred to me that I was in an on-again-off-again relationship — with my own voice. Maybe you can relate? Perhaps you feel as if you are tap-dancing on eggshells as you strive to be liked and to give the right answers. Or maybe you spend a lot of time hoping, with every cell in your body, that nobody will call you out for not being enough of whatever you conjecture other people want you to be.

And then at other times, sometimes in close proximity to those former times, you have an insufferable need to be recognized and praised for your achievements. You know you were born to make a big, positive impact on the world. And whether or not you believe you are on your way to leaving that legacy, you *do* know that you want to do more, say more, be more.

If you're thinking, *Oh, heck yes, that sounds a heckuva lot like me,* please know that you're not alone. For much of my life, even as I grew a business dishing out career and leadership advice to other women, I was insanely uncomfortable speaking up and being seen by the people around me. Simultaneously, and frustratingly, I was someone who pushed herself to excel. I entered

1

and won talent shows, scholarships, student council races, and even the Miss Junior America Pageant. Growing up with an abundance of love and a ton of privilege left me frequently feeling guilty and embarrassed, if not downright ashamed, for my feelings of not-enoughness, which rode shotgun next to my insatiable desire to perform like a dressage horse and win.

What I've learned through my work is that too many women, irrespective of our backgrounds and the privileges afforded us, are doing this super awkward Dr. Jekyll and Mr. Hyde routine. We flip-flop between demonstrating our supposed confidence and experiencing near-paralyzing insecurity. While we might fear that if we speak up we'll underwhelm or offend, the mental torture we put ourselves through is usually far worse than any communication coming from us.

A woman would need to have been stuck in a cryonics chamber for the past few years not to have been confronted with the litany of media, books, and courses telling her why she struggles with her confidence and influence — despite women in industrialized nations being more educated, earning more money, starting more businesses, and running for public office in greater numbers than ever before. Over the past few years, millions of women have spoken up on behalf of our rights and the rights of others. But it's one thing to show up to a march or broadcast your views in a social media post. It's an altogether different thing to tell yourself, and actually believe, that you possess the power and ability to advocate for yourself — especially if you are in an environment, professionally or personally, in which the people around you are complicit in maintaining the status quo. Media outlets such as CNN, PBS, and *Inc.* predicted that 2018 would be "the year of the woman," but how many of us really feel like we have the moxie we need to consistently speak up, tell our truth, and create the future we want for ourselves and our loved ones?

There has been no shortage of experts promising women tools for presenting our ideas more successfully, advocating for social change, and shifting our self-talk from self-critical to self-compassionate. Yet in conversations with my coaching clients, and with the smart, savvy entrepreneurial and professional women I meet through my presentations and trainings, I hear the same refrain over and over: *I can't stop my cray-cray self-talk — or the verbal vomit it often produces when I open my mouth to speak.*

Okay, not *exactly* their words, but you get the gist.

Despite how we might puff up and posture, too many of us are powering through our lives with wretched self-confidence, and we are not fulfilling our potential or squeezing all the juice out of our lives as a result. We are overdue for a new paradigm for our empowerment, one that recognizes the impact of sexism, racism, classism, and all the other *isms* that have not gone away — and in many cases are actively being stoked. A paradigm that provides a holistic pathway for each of us to (re)claim our voices. For if we are to speak up and out for ourselves, and the many causes that require our championship, our pathway forward must enable us to cultivate the mindset and behaviors to transform our communication with ourselves so that we can transform the communication we put out into the world.

What Do You Mean by *Moxie*, Lex?

The word *moxie* has become synonymous with *vigor, verve, pep, courage, nerve, aggressiveness, skill,* and *know-how.* While the word didn't come into common use until the 1930s in the United States, with the advent of Moxie soda, it can be traced back to 1876, when Dr. Augustin Thompson, Moxie's founder, first created and marketed "Moxie Nerve Food," a medicine that he claimed treated paralysis, nervousness, and insomnia. I acknowledge that those claims sound as dubious as my preschool-aged daughter's when she tells me her dad told her she could have another thirty minutes of screen time. (Although well done, Dr. Thompson, for successfully persuading many of your contemporaries to believe your theory — and for securing a medical patent for your concoction and successfully building the Moxie soda brand!)

I love the word *moxie* because it suggests a way of thinking, a way of feeling, and a way of behaving that activates speaking up and disrupting the status quo. This is what *Step into Your Moxie* is all about — amplifying your voice, visibility, and influence in the world — even if, especially if, you have previously struggled to do so in your work, your community, and your personal life. My desire, during our journey together, is for you to discover, and never forget, that you can walk into any room, or onto any stage, and speak with moxie — and inspire other people to do the same.

In my midtwenties, when I first decided I wanted to be a coach, one of my coaching instructors asked, "What's the question you were born to answer?" As everyone around me started scribbling his or her responses, I felt like a kid lost in a theme park — small, overwhelmed, and in need of some grown-up direction. Yet, as I made a habit of doing most of my life, I said nothing. I smiled, nodded my head, and I'm pretty sure even moaned a little — *hmm, uh-huh, yeah* — so that nobody could see how much of a phony-boloney I felt like inside. Then, a few years later, having hung out my shingle as a coach and launched a semisuccessful career as a motivational workplace speaker, I found my answer. Or rather, my answer found me.

I arrived a bit early to a social innovation conference where I was the closing keynote speaker, in time to catch the participants' pitch fest. Each of the approximately one hundred twentysomethings in attendance had a couple of minutes to present their big idea for how to harness entrepreneurial solutions to solve a big social, economic, or environmental problem. The pitches rocked.

They were bold, well researched, and full of heart. The speakers presented their ideas in front of fellow attendees, and everyone present voted for who they felt gave the best pitch. When the finalists' names were announced, I was incredulous, for every single one of those named was male. In a room full of approximately fifty young men and fifty young women, not one woman was selected by her peers.

As I do whenever I'm a little riled up, and I was steamier than a boiling teapot that day, I started to ask anybody who would listen to me, "What happened? Where are the voices of our women?" And what I learned surprised me, sobered me, and enabled me to find what had been an elusive answer to the question about my life purpose.

Both the male and female participants told me they had voted based on who they perceived to be the best speaker. In other words, who spoke up, projected confidence, took up space, owned their accomplishments, exuded charm and charisma — a masculine model of influence. And yet when I asked, "Who were the speakers that you felt most connected to? That you trusted? That made you want to really get involved in solving the issue they illuminated?" both the young men and women mentioned the names of female participants. They concurred that many of the female speakers shared stories that stirred the heart and the soul. They engendered trust as they told the truth about themselves, at times even confessing they still had a lot to learn before they felt their ideas could have the full impact they wanted. This, however, was not deemed effective communication.

That's when I knew I felt like a bull in the ring who's just seen a red cape, because I've been in *that* audience most of my life. I've discounted my communication as a woman, my inner voice, and I've evaluated my success based on a masculine model that normalizes confidence, assertiveness, authority, and taking up space — qualities I always felt I had in short supply. I want to step into my moxie, I told myself. I want to speak my passion, assert my perspectives, and be humble and honest, and I want to do it Sinatra style — *my way*. I want to integrate the masculine and the feminine so that I can argue on behalf of ideas, claim space for myself and my ideas, tell stories, ask questions, make people laugh, and when appropriate, make them cry. *That* is what I'm born to do. The question I am born to answer: *How can I show other people, particularly women, how to do the same?*

Fewer than ninety days after that life-changing and life-charging pitch fest, I rebaptized myself as a women's speaking and leadership coach — and I haven't looked back. Through my individual and group coaching and training programs, keynote speeches, seminars, and retreats, I've supported tens of thousands of executives, entrepreneurs, coaches, healers, change agents, and emerging leaders to speak with power and impact at work, in business, with their friends and family, onstage, on camera, and above all, to themselves. And the word *moxie* has stuck. After a writer in the White House Office of Public Engagement referred to me as a "Moxie Maven" for my women's empowerment work, I became more intentional about referring to my calling as empowering women to step into their moxie.

Are You My Reader? I Think...Yes!

I'm not totally sure why you picked up this book. Maybe you had a rough childhood that sent you down a path of lousy self-esteem and sorely lacking self-worth. Or you've experienced racism, classism, or everyday gender bias that has had a profound impact on your sense of personal power — or lack thereof. It's also possible that you have enjoyed heaps of privilege, that people around you have consistently lauded your talents, and that you have no idea why, more often than you care to admit, you default to apologizing when you've done nothing wrong, hedge when you share your opinions, and say to yourself (and possibly others), "I'm not ready" when opportunities present themselves. If any of the above sounds familiar, know that I've got you, sista. Or brotha. (While you've probably figured out by now that I did write this book for women, if you are male, trans, or gender questioning and you've made it thus far, I'm confident that with an open mind and an even more open heart you'll be able to extract and apply the principles I share as well.)

And don't worry, you've also picked up the right book if you've got boatloads of moxie — if you love asking for the money you're worth, holding a mic in your hand, and calling people to action. If you routinely step into your moxie, this book will give you an opportunity to stretch into more authenticity, pleasure, and ease in your communication so you can elicit the maximum possible buy-in for your ideas, enhance your connection with others, and sustain your influence.

Over the course of thirteen chapters, I merge stories that have prompted big communication discoveries for me with simple, effective, and practical recommendations so you can take these lessons, apply them, and experience deep and lasting transformation in all facets of your communication. You'll discover how to adopt the role of protagonist in the story you have created about who you are as a communicator. From making new, self-empowering choices in your self-talk, to using communication that catalyzes your power and influence, to harnessing your intuition and speaking what you were born to say, you'll develop the foundation to step into your moxie in all areas of your life.

I'll also show you how to take your communication into the world, be it through daring conversations, negotiations, or presentations. You will buff up the muscles for having unshakable presence when the spotlight is on you, and compile tools to navigate through the inevitable "feels" that come up when creating greater visibility for yourself and your ideas. I'll show you how to step into your moxie even when it feels like the universe, and everyone in it, is slapping you with constraints rather than blessing you with what I affectionately refer to as cosmic winks — signs that you are on the right track and can keep going. You'll create and learn to articulate your boundaries to the people in your life. You'll know how to rise and be resilient in the face of setbacks and to speak up and out for the causes that matter most to you — so that you can leave the legacy you were born to create.

I'll also help you lighten up and stop taking your communication, and yourself, so seriously. I want to show you that stepping into your moxie can be simple and fun — so that you're not afraid to do it. And in the moments when you pivot back to old, not-so-moxieful ways of speaking to and for yourself and others, you'll quickly shake it off, recalibrate, and come back into your power. For when you have more fun with your communication, you will stop censoring yourself and hustling for others' approval and praise. You will by default speak *your* truth — with kindness, compassion, and ease. You'll see using your voice as an act of divine service to yourself and to the world.

I wrote this book for you (and me) to read, cover to cover, again and again. Before you ask for that promotion. Hop on the phone with a prospective client. Tell your honey you want all in to (or on the flip side, to get the heck out of) your relationship. I want you to come back and pick up *Step into Your Moxie* as you contemplate raising your hand for a prestigious opportunity, as you prepare to deliver a game-changing presentation, and above all, whenever you psychically whip yourself for something you said (or failed to speak out against). Also, my precious reader, this book is not just about you. I want you to pay it forward and use your voice and influence to reshape policies and practices you disagree with so they more accurately reflect your values — at work, in your community, around the world, and in your family. Moxie is not just what you do with your voice — it's also what you leave behind through your influence.

I encourage you (okay, let me be more forthcoming, *implore you*) to do the Moxie Moment exercises in each chapter. I want you to develop the behaviors and habits to put your new moxie mindset into action. I also hope you'll check out the downloadable worksheets, meditations, and other recommended resources I've created for you at AlexiaVernon.com/MoxieBook. This is where you can join my *Step into Your Moxie* virtual family and connect with other readers from around the world. My online communities attract some powerhouse people. Come on over and see!

One Final Thought, Then Let's Do This

I started writing this book right around the time I left my first and last full-time job in order to be a coach. Concurrently, I was supplementing my initially paltry coaching income by teaching women's studies and public speaking at local universities. I had no business doling out advice on much of anything then. Yet on my lengthy subway, bus, and light-rail rides between university gigs, I started scribbling down notes and compiling stories I wanted to share, many of which have made it into the book you are reading. In hindsight, I know I was writing the book I needed to read. As you'll hear me say a few more times, we teach what we need to learn and, often, what we need to remember.

Fast-forward a little more than a decade later, and I've learned some things. And I promise you that if you show up, keep turning the pages, curtail your judgments about yourself (and, if you need to, about others), and commit yourself to applying the principles in this book, you will step into your moxie. You will default to speaking your truth. Championing yourself and others. Claiming the visibility that your ideas and your work deserve. And you will create the legacy you were born to leave.

Wherever you are on your moxie trajectory, whether you are at the start of your career, at the midpoint, or winding down, I invite you to stay open, do the work (seriously, *do the work in each chapter* — don't be too cool to grow and evolve), and take your discoveries and put them into action. If you find a story, question, exercise, or recommendation triggering, poke around and see why before discounting it or skipping over it.

What might the discomfort be there to teach you?

How might it be beckoning you to stretch?

Heal?

Forgive?

How might it even be shining a light on a question, *the question*, you were born to answer?

This wacky, wonderful world we live in — it needs your voice. It needs your wisdom. And your wit. So while I get that you will likely need to navigate some external, real-world limitations, and some self-imposed ones, to step into your moxie, let's get to making moxie a lifelong habit. You with me?

1

HEADGEAR, HAIRY LEGS, AND
A QUARTER LIFE OF HUMILIATION

*It takes years as a woman to unlearn what you have been taught
to be sorry for. It takes years to find your voice and seize your real
estate.*

— AMY POEHLER

By the time I was in the third grade, my teeth were a disaster.
I had sucked my thumb since shortly after busting out of my
mother's womb, so by the dawn of my tween years I had a serious
overbite, a shallow palate, and heaps of crooked teeth. My mom
and orthodontist were in cahoots. They wanted immediate and
aggressive action.

First, since I had a tongue thrust, I received a…wait for it…
tongue thrust corrector. A couple of metal spikes were put into a
device that was then lodged into my upper palate. Its purpose? To
cut my tongue each time it came forward and teach it to stay in
the back of my mouth.

Second, we had to treat my overbite. In my upper palate, another device was implanted to realign my jaw. It had a spot for a key, and a couple of times a day I would turn this key to bring my jaw back into its proper place.

Third, I got braces. Because what kid has ever gone to the orthodontist and not been told she needs braces? (Also, I feel it's important for you to know, I thought it would be really cool to match the rubber bands on my braces with my glasses, so for a couple of years, between my eyes and mouth, I was rocking a lot of turquoise.)

And last, but most certainly not least, I was gifted with headgear. As you are visualizing, be sure you don't mistakenly picture headgear's slightly more attractive cousin, neck gear, which you could pretty effectively mask if you had long hair like I always have. Nope, I got the silly-looking strappy hat contraption which, even though it was pitched to me as blending in with my hair, most certainly did not.

So, to recap — tongue thrust corrector, jaw realigner, braces, and headgear. Shortly after my postapocalyptic makeover I was tasked with giving my first speech, a current-events presentation. I dreaded this day like a toddler dreads bedtime. Only substitute a tantrum for paralysis and alcohol withdrawal–like shakes.

When the day arrived, everything felt as if it was happening in slow motion. The twenty minutes of presentations that preceded mine might as well have been twenty hours. When it was finally my turn to speak, I made my way up to the front of the room and looked out at the sea of faces in my third-grade classroom. I took a deep breath, opened my mouth to start, and…nothing came out through my metal accoutrement.

Okay, that's not entirely true. A nice visible driblet of drool did.

I closed my eyes. I took another deep breath, and as I attempted to begin again I realized that my classmates were now rocking in their seats, shaking, really, as they tried to suppress their mounting laughter. At me.

By this point my heart was beating so loudly I'm pretty sure it was heard a zip code or two or twenty away. I could feel the sweat running down my arms, and my knees knocking together, and meanwhile my words were still utterly trapped. Finally, I got something out, despite my quaky voice, and waded through the rest of the speech I'd prepared. Now all my classmates were audibly laughing, my tears were flowing — definitely with more ease than my words had — and I vowed that I would *never* put myself in a position where I could feel humiliated like that again. Sadly, that didn't work out, but not from lack of effort.

I didn't make a conscious decision that day to start disappearing. To rarely raise my voice for fear of shaking up the status quo. To overplease and behind the scenes seek to overperform. What I know with absolute certainty, however, is that as a result of that first, brutal speech I created a story for myself that I was a lousy public speaker. For too many years, whenever I had to get up to talk in front of a group of people, heck, many times when I was merely answering a question, I suffered from heart palpitations, body sweats, and self-talk so nasty it would have made Amy Schumer blush.

And of course, as stories are known to do, mine created my reality. Without fail, when I opened my mouth to speak, a part of me would time-travel back to that first speech, my voice would quaver, my body would shake, I would feel myself turning red, and often I would cry. And each time this happened, I wrote and later archived another chapter in my running narrative about my lousy communication abilities.

But alas, the more I feared humiliation, the more I excelled at attracting it. From accidentally peeing onstage during a dance recital to falling and breaking my arm in the middle of a school carnival, most days I felt like I was competing against myself for the Most Embarrassing Moment Award. And I kept on winning.

Then, the summer between sixth and seventh grade, I went to Space Academy. And things got even *hairier*. I was into math and science, so my dad had called the fine folks at Space Academy and told them, despite my age, which made me a better candidate for their younger Space Camp program, that because of my straight As, and my fierce work ethic, they should make an exception and let me join the older kids. Access granted.

I loved Space Academy, for about half a day. At the start of the program we took a test to determine our roles in an ongoing mock mission. When we got our test results back shortly after, I learned I had scored middle of the pack — impressive, given that I was testing alongside kids one, two, in some cases three years my senior. Not impressive, however, for a twelve-year-old whose self-worth was inextricably connected to her academic performance.

My score, or lack thereof, meant that I spent the rest of my four days in activities with the other "average" students — who happened to be the cool girls. Most of them had long blond hair — magically untouched by the Huntsville humidity that was making my brown hair look like I was camping without a tent in a hurricane. They rocked sinfully sweet Southern accents, and they had legs way smoother than mine. We'll come back to that.

While to my face my girl crewmates dripped with kindness, every time they had to pick a mission buddy, they picked me last. In the dining hall, the first girl through the food line always managed to save a seat for everyone but yours truly. Then there was the night in my room when the girl in the bunk below me pulled a Swiss Army knife on the girl in the opposite bunk and I peed all over myself in bed while pretending to be asleep. Fortunately, my sleep performance was compelling enough that nobody noticed. (And while this episode has zero bearing on where we are headed,

I'm throwing it in so you can appreciate why I stayed as far away from a science classroom as possible once I got home. Girl crew plus blade plus another unintended peeing mishap equaled "I hate science" in my tween head.)

Fast-forward to the last day of Space Academy. Everybody in my girl crew was exchanging her Academy yearbook, and every time I asked if somebody would sign mine, I was greeted with a painfully overenthusiastic, "Of course!" Yet nobody asked me to sign her yearbook in return. The good news is that by lunch I had figured out why. The bad news is — by lunch I had figured out why.

That final day I decided I would do anything to sit with the girl crew, so at lunch I skipped the food line, went to their table, and put my yearbook down next to the other ones that were reserving seats. And that's when I saw it. The inside joke that had bonded the girl crew together. Next to my picture was a note, *the note*, that revealed all.

Had so much fun. We'll always remember our Little Hairy Beast!

Simply typing the words *Little Hairy Beast* today feels as much like a sucker punch to the soul as it did when reading those words back then. Except when I was pregnant, I've been pencil thin my entire life, and I was lucky to escape the body shame so many adolescent girls experience, and perpetually experience, once they curve and fold in new ways. But being called hairy and discovering I hadn't been oversensitive, that I had in fact been ostracized, also emboldened me. Unlike my friends, who often felt enslaved as their bodies betrayed them, I realized I could do something immediately about my beastliness.

When I got home early the next day, I promptly went into my mother's bathroom, grabbed her razor, and shaved every inch of hair (and at least a few centimeters of skin) off my legs. Over the next year, I'd shave my armpits. Then my arms. Then the stray hairs above my upper lip. I won't keep going, but you should know. I. Did. Keep. Going.

My current-events speech, complete with headgear, was humiliating because I performed badly. Space Academy was humiliating because of the mistreatment, sure, but also, and more important, because of who I concluded I was. Or wasn't. Therefore, like an addict who transcends her pain every time she gets high, through my teen years and into much of my twenties, I similarly got addicted to my version of emotional numbness. I would temporarily rid myself of my congenital beastliness (thank you, Eastern European Jewish father and Greek mother) by shaving my body hair. But of course, within a couple of days, the hair always grew back. And with it came a new wave of self-hatred — and a desire to disappear that no amount of shaving could absolve me from.

Thankfully, although I had a codependent relationship with my razor until my midtwenties, when a couple of guy friends staged an intervention, my high school and college years were considerably less humiliating. (Although when I won the Miss Junior America Pageant at nineteen, I froze a little too long after hearing my name called because I was wondering, *Are the cameras from* America's Funniest Home Videos *here for a gotcha moment?* It was that inconceivable to me that even freshly shaven I could win the one and only beauty competition I had ever entered.)

The Birthplace of Moxie

What I know from telling stories like these during my keynotes, and from sharing them privately with clients who are struggling with their own visibility, is that as wackadoodle as I can be, my inner monologues were not, are not, aberrations. They are actually the norm. Sometimes our worst visibility fears do come true. People laugh when we speak. Or tell us that we are wrong. That we're not smart. Attractive. Funny. Or deserving of a seat at the table.

Whenever I speak with clients or audience members about their communication, I'm struck by how almost every one of them (even those like me who had a phenomenal education and a ton of privilege or who I *know* were the kids laughing at class-mates' speeches and gossiping behind so-called friends' backs) has had a headgear or a hairy-beast moment. And as a result has slipped into a self-defeating narrative about who they are and their potential to use their voices in the world.

But can I let you in on the truly heartbreaking part?

Most people allow how they perceive their own voices to be determined by one or two moments in their histories. That moment when they spoke up and didn't get the response they wanted. Or stayed mum and allowed something unjust to happen. Those fleeting moments have become the stories they replay, often unconsciously, over and over again. And I get it. I did, and sometimes still do, the same thing — despite the many moments in my life when I have been more than moxieful.

What story have you been carrying around about who you are as a communicator?

Give yourself an opportunity to sit with that question for as long as you need to. Journal on it. It's an important one. For until you know the narrative that underpins how you talk to yourself, nothing I tell you about how to step into your moxie will mat-ter — because it will be treating the symptom rather than going to the source of what's standing between you and the consistent, empowered use of your voice in the world.

Then it's time to assess your story. And I don't just mean in terms of its validity. Whether your story is true, kind of true, remarkably untrue, or somewhere in between, ask yourself:

Is that story setting me up to show up, speak up, and be seen in the world?

I recommend that you go back to your journal and free-write on this too. Because if your answer is anything other than an unequivocal *holy yes*, it's time for a rewrite. For the way we communicate with ourselves fundamentally shapes the way we communicate in all facets of our life. I know, not rocket science. Which is fortunate, because as you also know, my hairy legs precluded a career in science.

Here, however, is the bigger story. The meat and potatoes — or for my plant-based friends, the kale and quinoa — of it all. It's possible to shift your internal communication so that the self-talk that arises, moment to moment, sets you up to think, feel, and speak from a place of moxie. The problem is that most of us attempt to address our self-talk without doing the deeper dive into identifying the story (or stories) that trigger the self-talk in the first place. As a result, we might tell ourselves affirmations like:

My inner beauty creates my outer beauty.

I've got this.

I am the hero I've been waiting for.

I am a vessel for love.

My flatulence makes me powerful.

While these words in and of themselves are not necessarily flawed, they usually don't stick. And sometimes, unfortunately, they actually prompt us to communicate and act in ways that undermine our moxie. They can make us want to puff up and project a confidence that is ego- rather than heart-driven. They can make us pursue external success, thinking if we simply check off more items from an achievement list, then moxie will finally be ours. As a result, we hustle harder for other people's approval — losing more and more connection to our authentic voice along the way.

Let's stop doing this, uttering words we haven't created the context to believe, psychically stabbing ourselves for failing to believe them, and then abusing ourselves by going out and behaving in ways that don't serve our highest good. Instead, let's go deep — and delicious. Let's identify and release the stories that are giving rise to the most important communication we do in the world — the communication with ourselves.

Find Your "Come to Jesus" Moments

Before we go any further, please know that what I'm about to ask you to do has as much to do with Jesus as Christmas often does. And please know, I love me some Jesus. And God. Our conversations have gotten me through some dark, complicated times — many of which I'll invite you into as we continue our journey together. But if the Big J, God, or religion freak you out, or run counter to your beliefs, make what I'm suggesting work for *you*, and don't scrunch your face up and get all hot and bothered over terminology.

When I invite you to consider your Come to Jesus moments, what I'm requesting is that you identify moments in your life that brought you to your knees, humbled you, made you surrender, and in hindsight (because during them you undoubtedly were miserable), you know played a role in cultivating your voice, strength, and resilience — even if you haven't always (maybe not ever) seen these times this way. Whether you are Greek Orthodox, as I was raised, Jewish like my pops, Buddhist, Muslim, Hindu, agnostic, or anything else, I'm confident you've had moments that have tested your faith — at least in yourself. This is what I want you to mine.

Okay, no more disclaimers. Let's do this. And seriously, *do this*, and all the other Moxie Moment exercises that I share. I want you to get the aha's you picked up this book for! (If you prefer to download the companion worksheet, visit AlexiaVernon.com /MoxieBook.)

THE FIVE Rs
(Recall, Relive, Reframe, Release, and Reapply)

Directions: Identify three to five significant experiences ("Come to Jesus" moments) that have shaped how you think of yourself, your voice, your presence, and your purpose. First, in your journal (or in your downloadable worksheet), you are going to **Recall** these pivotal experiences. On the left side of the page, list them, naming each one so that you know what it represents. Next to this name, on the right, you are going to list some basic details of what happened as you **Relive** (or reexperience) the journey you went through — as I did with my current-events and Space Academy stories. Don't worry; I won't leave you in Relive for very long. But you have to go into your story to get through it and heal it.

Now that you have Recalled and Relived, you are going to pick the one or two experiences you feel are most relevant to you (who you are and who you are striving to become). For each, you will write your **Reframe**. This is where you will begin to shift from seeing what happened *to* you as something that happened *for* you — to help you learn, grow, and cultivate resilience. While I certainly wasn't grateful for the embarrassing and diminishing moments I shared with you earlier in the chapter, I have reframed them and now see them as moments that prepared me for my work as a coach, speaker, and author. Identify how you can consciously see your experience so that it empowers your voice and presence — rather than undermining it (or you). And again, be sure to write it down.

To ensure that your Reframe for each experience really sticks, you need to now **Release** it. At this stage, you let go of any thoughts, feelings, beliefs, and habits that are getting in the way of truly believing your Reframes. In your journal or worksheet, write the word *Release*, and list anything and everything that you are letting go of, once and for all. For me this would include a desire to publicly shame any of my childhood humiliators or to travel back in time and give an Oscar Award–winning presentation. Feel free to combine your experiences as you cull together everything you want to release.

In the final R, **Reapply**, you identify how you have carried forward and how you will continue to carry forward the knowledge awakened in the Reframe section. Try not to list just what you have done / will do (e.g., the behaviors or actions) but also the evidence you will look for, or perhaps already possess, that proves you are embodying your Reframe(s) in all spheres of your life. Writing this book is a *huge* piece of my Reapply!

QUESTIONS FOR REFLECTION

- As you look back on your work in the five Rs, what are you discovering?
- What role have your stories played in the development of your inner and outer voice?
- What will the payoff be for holding your Reframes and Releases and committing to your Reapplies?
- What other truer, more self-empowering stories could you be telling?
- What would it cost you if you went back and lingered in the Recall and Relive of your old story (or stories)?

Make Moxie a Lifelong Habit

Once you illuminate the stories that have created a glass ceiling for your moxie, you have the power to shatter them. How? By making a new habit of telling better stories that reinforce who you *are* versus who you are *not*. Then and only then can you begin to address your self-talk, the sensation you experience when you speak up, and your actual speaking performance.

Just as I don't remember the exact moment when I started to disappear, I also don't recall quite when and how I started speaking up again. It happened in fits and starts. Having parents who told me I could do anything I set my mind to, and going to a progressive all-girls secondary school that every day reminded me that my voice mattered, certainly helped. So did winning that pageant and subsequently becoming a youth motivational speaker. However, without learning how to rewrite my self-narrative or correcting my poor speaking habits, I was unable to ten-thousand-hours my way to lasting, unwavering speaking confidence — particularly when I had an audience beyond my peers. The first time I locked eyes with a junior high boy who looked disinterested in one of my teen empowerment audiences, all the old gremlins came back. And they were on steroids.

And so it went, from my late teens into my midtwenties. As an actor, I could get onstage and do a one-and-a-half-hour one-woman performance of Joan of Arc. As a trainer, I could facilitate professional development for teachers. I was effin' brilliant whenever I got to hide behind a character or my expertise. But in the moments when I was truly being seen by others, like when I'd strive to articulate a potentially unpopular opinion to a supervisor or introduce myself at a theater audition to a casting director, I'd become a bumbling mess all over again. And the real bumbling, of course, happened in my inner monologues when I rehashed, and then beat myself up, afterward. Over. And over. Again.

What I want, my precious reader, is for you to become the heroine of your own narrative. I'm not interested in whether you turn that idea, or anything else that I share, into a cheesy affirmation. I want you to possess the moxie to actually make it happen. I want you to learn, practice, and master the inner and outer work necessary to speak with confidence and competence whenever you open your mouth. And along the way, I want you to stop worrying about whether you are getting it right. Because a lot of the time, you won't be. And that's okay. What's considerably less okay is replaying your flops at the expense of forgetting your successes. I speak what it's taken me most of my lifetime to learn. And remember.

I also really want you to unhook from the persistent drizzle of anxiety you (if you are like most ambitious, overachieving women I know and serve) carry with you throughout your life. People may laugh at you. They may call you names. You may pee on yourself. Multiple times. And you will survive. So please, take a moment and answer this very serious question:

What's the worst thing that could happen if you consistently spoke your truth?

And once you answer it, ask yourself the equally important follow-up question:

And then what would happen?

And keep asking yourself this same follow-up question (and writing down your responses) until you can't go any further. For example, you might find yourself writing:

People would lose respect for me.
I'd be out of a job.

I'd struggle to pay my mortgage.

I'd have to move in with my crazy Aunt Zelda and take care of her seven cats.

I'd have to subsist on ramen noodles (the ones in a package, not the swanky noodle shop kind).

I mean, you pretty quickly realize that there might be some situational suckiness, but you'd survive, right? So tango with your worst truth telling, visibility, and speaking fears. By going to the worst-case scenario, you liberate yourself to start considering what else might happen.

What's the best-case scenario if you stepped into your moxie? Or even the pretty okay, albeit not totally perfect, scenario?

You mitigate anxiety by calling out, and having a plan in place for, the potential fallout from speaking up. But your other equally important, delicious work is to invest your time, energy, and sweat into setting yourself up for all the beautiful things that can happen when you are able to listen to, honor, and speak from your moxie. Habitually.

In the next chapter, I'll show you how to identify the specific voices you hear in your head — and help you discern which are empowering your moxie and which are sabotaging it. Then I'll give you a foolproof process for evicting the voices that have overstayed their welcome so that you can fill your precious mental real estate with a more loving, moxie-inducing presence.

2

CRITICS, COPS, AND CHEERLEADERS...OH MY!

People often say that motivation doesn't last. Well, neither does bathing — that's why we recommend it daily.

— ZIG ZIGLAR

Two weeks before my sixteenth birthday, my grandma passed away from pneumonia. The year proceeding her death was one of the darkest periods of my life. I got my first B+ in a math class, due to missing several weeks of school while I sat bedside with my grandma hoping, in vain, that she would come off her respirator prior to her death. Integrating the reality that I may not be as Andrea Zuckerman *90210* smart as I'd been led to believe with the reality that I would have to live the majority of my life without one of my favorite humans, was a bullet train ride into depression for me. And as a theater student, I went big. I plotted what I could do with a bottle of over-the-counter pain pills I had in a medicine cabinet, went on a long drive (because I was too physically and emotionally depleted to consider running away from home), and was prescribed a series of antidepressants (and even a mood stabilizer) — none of which could pull me out of my funk.

Before this episode, I might have been typecast in the role of Sally Sunshinepants. (Don't bother looking up that reference. It's not a thing, but it should be.) Sure, I could slide into teen-girl angst from time to time, but overall I defaulted to seeing the positive in most people, places, and things — even while I trudged through some objectively awful experiences. But something happened after my grandma's death. I stopped working so hard to manage the voices in my head. Instead, when life gave me lemons — in small, mundane ways like getting a mosquito bite, not getting the parking spot I wanted, or being left at prom by my date (okay, that wasn't quite so mundane. I think my freak-out was pretty justified in that instance) — I ate the lemon and then ruminated on why it was so dang sour going down. In other words, I chose to speak to myself in a way that set me up to feel miserable.

The Orchestra in the Head

At any given moment, most of us are strolling around with one of three voices prattling on in our heads. None of them is really us, and none of them is setting us up for inner or outer communication success. While the presence of self-talk, and the impact it has on how you think, feel, and behave is likely not a new concept for you, if these voices still exist for you and, more important, if you are struggling to manage them, well, then, we need to address them. In this chapter, we'll jam on how to talk *back* to them — since they play such a profound role in how we show up and speak up.

The first voice that might be hanging out in your noggin is the voice of the Critic. She's an unapologetic mean girl. She's also not very creative. She sets you up to perpetually feel like you are an impostor in your own life and gives you unwanted immunity against your own greatness.

She says things like:

You're not smart enough.

You're not pretty enough.

You're not experienced enough.

You don't smile enough.

You don't have a big enough network.

You're not skinny enough.

You're not curvy enough.

You're not hairless enough.

Okay, maybe that last one is just *my* Critic speaking.

When the Critic in your head holds the mic, you never believe you are enough. You doubt your decisions and the choices you have before you. And, above all, you feel as if in every moment the world is seeing you as a contestant on a reality TV show the minute she lands in the bottom two — and everyone watching, including the contestant, knows she's about to lose and be voted off. When you let (because it is always a choice) a chatty Critic run the show, you live in your head, disassociate from your body and spirit, and often censor your outer voice — believing that nobody wants to hear what you have to say.

I lead a mastermind group for female entrepreneurs and changemakers who want to use speaking to spread their ideas, grow their businesses, and make a positive impact on the world. The participating women all have the opportunity to film speaker reels and receive photographs of themselves onstage speaking.

I see these women's Critics show up big-time during this process. Whether a woman is in her late twenties, nearing her golden years, or somewhere in between, the feedback she provides my team when reviewing her materials is rarely related to her speaking content — or even to her performance. What we hear in spades are comments like:

My roots are showing.

My face looks like a drawing on an Etch A Sketch. Can the elevens between my eyes be Photoshopped?

Why didn't you tell me a wrap dress makes me look like a ruptured pork sausage?

Now, these women are doing significant work in the world, in many cases not only changing but literally saving people's lives. Many are active in women's empowerment, and yet when they view themselves speaking, what they consistently see are their blemishes rather than their beauty marks.

Unfortunately, the Critic is not the only voice that likes to eat up our mental and emotional bandwidth and compromise our communication success. She has a bestie, whom I affectionately refer to as the Cop. And the Cop, as Cops are wont to do, polices your decision making and turns everything into a dichotomy. In other words, there are a maximum of two options in any situation — and they are at odds with each other.

There are good people and bad people.

There's the right vocation; all others are my karmic mismatch.

I can be a rock star, or I can be the roadie.

When our Cop directs the show in our heads, she strives to make everything black-and-white. Sinful or sacred. As a result, we forget that most of life exists in the gray, too often underused, space between these extremes. So much discourse in the world right now is mean, one-sided, one-note, and judgmental. When we have a Cop in our heads, we inevitably are too.

When I began my coaching business, I worked with a lot of twenty- and thirtysomethings who were in the throes of career transition. Many of my clients were habitually changing jobs, as my generation is inclined to do. In some cases, they switched jobs after only six months, or less. One woman, whom I'll call Ruby, was one such client.

I met Ruby at one of my facilitation workshops. At the time, she had a university leadership position, and she felt stymied by all the institutional bureaucracy. She wanted more substantive face time with students, and she sought tools for facilitating deeper transformation — and this is how she found herself in one of my workshops. When we began working together, she quickly decided she could never have what she wanted in the environment she was in, so she took the opportunity (and a financial step backward) to manage transformational programs for a holistic center in a rural community. Within less than a month in this new role, Ruby felt she had made a terrible mistake. She missed her friends, she missed her coworkers, and she missed living in a big city. And although she loved the vision and mission of her new employer, she felt even further away from her goal of facilitating transformation now that she was a manager and had little interaction with people, outside her small team. Ruby decided to take the first opportunity she could get back in her old city as a departmental administrator, and in doing so, also took her second demotion in less than a year.

When you are a coach, your agenda is always supposed to be your client's agenda, but I'll be honest, I had my own agenda for Ruby, though I wasn't experienced or brave enough to articulate it at the time. I wanted her to realize the role her Cop-like self-talk played in her somewhat manic job-hopping. Ruby, like so many other perfection-seeking women, kept telling herself there was a *right* job for her — and that everything else was dead *wrong*. As a result, the minute she didn't feel cozy in a new opportunity, she bailed, for she interpreted her discomfort as a sign that she was fundamentally off purpose. Instead of living and learning through an experience that was happening *for* her, she interpreted the situation as happening *to* her. She also barely moved the needle when negotiating either of her offers — which, while shocking, given that she had taught negotiation workshops, makes sense. She was so mired in her Cop thinking, she had a hard time coming up with creative alternatives to money when her employers failed to concede more than a few thousand dollars on their offers.

In addition to the voices of the Critic and Cop, there is a third, equally self-sabotaging voice. Unlike the Critic and Cop, this voice is usually pretty positive — she is a bit of a frenemy. This voice is the Cheerleader. The Cheerleader is, as the name suggests, extremely adept at cheering you on. She tells you:

I'm cool with my client's passive-aggressive emails.

I can pull a second consecutive all-nighter to get that financial report done.

It's fine that I have a big presentation in an hour, my partner is out of town, and my kiddo's school just called to ask me to come pick her up because she's got a raging fever. I'll figure it out. Always do.

Now, in all fairness, the Cheerleader voice, in moderation, isn't such a bad thing. In moments when we have to bulldoze through something uncomfortable and necessary — our first week at a new job, a negotiation, an illness (ours or somebody else's), or telling a tantrum-prone kiddo to put her stickers away — we definitely want to empower this voice. However, when we go to her by default rather than by design, ultimately we are going to feel frustrated and tired. It's going to make us feel like we are playing hopscotch on hot coals, and we are going to get sick, wear out, and step *out* of our moxie because we aren't addressing the real issues in our lives. Usually, it means that while we appear almost clown-like, with a smile painted across our faces, inside — even if we are in denial about it to ourselves — we're one trigger away from unraveling. And when we do, we often verbally flog the person or people closest to us.

That's why my grandma's death jump-started such a scary, seemingly bottomless downward spiral for me. Yes, we were bonded at the hip (and ankle and ear — and everywhere in between). Yet in hindsight, I realize that her passing also killed off my Cheerleader voice. I couldn't tell myself, *Everything will be fine*, because without my grandma in my life there was a ginormous chasm and nothing, especially me, felt like it would be fine again. Up until this point, my identity was also completely enmeshed in my academic achievement and artistic performance. That B+ started a chain reaction of tectonic movement. But just like a volcano that often erupts in the aftermath of a big quake, the lava (in my case my Cheerleader-like self-talk, which had been masking a lack of intrinsic worthiness), had been building for years.

For each of these voices — and to be sure, many of us (yours truly included) are blessed with an ability to house a Critic, a Cop, and sometimes even a Cheerleader simultaneously — the solution is the same.

We must develop the right, succinct messaging to talk back to ourselves in the voice of the Coach.

Wait, what?!

Yes, we're inviting another voice into our mental menagerie. But before I unmask her, let me explain why she's necessary.

Many of us strive to hit the mute button on our self-talk. We erroneously believe that if we put a muzzle on our Critic, Cop, or Cheerleader we can force her into submission and reconnect with our real voice, with our moxie. But as we explored in the previous chapter, it's not enough to pump ourselves up with affirmations or meditative and visualization practices designed to enhance our capacity for presence. Our Critics, Cops, and Cheerleaders are piping up in response to an underlying problem that must be addressed. And until it is, any and all efforts to quiet these voices

— well, they will be as successful as telling ourselves, *I'll just have one scoop of ice cream.* That might work if you are in an ice-cream store. But if you are at home, in less than five minutes, one scoop usually leads to an empty pint and a bloated belly. And so it is with our self-talk. When we say to ourselves, *Stop it. Use your theater voice,* our self-talk whispers turn into the finale of act 1 in *The Phantom of the Opera* (when the chandelier crashes to the floor).

How Our Self-Talk Impacts Our Moxie

Our communication with ourselves has a profound impact on how we feel, how we behave, and ultimately how we speak up in the world. In her book *My Stroke of Insight: A Brain Scientist's Personal Journey*, neuroanatomist Jill Bolte Taylor (who at the pinnacle of her career had a stroke and worked for eight years to fully recover her physical functioning and thinking abilities), writes provocatively not only about her own harrowing experience but also about the direct relationship between our thoughts and our feelings. And by feelings I (and Dr. Jill) don't just mean whether we are happy, sad, scared, angry, or bewildered but also how we physiologically feel in our bodies.

As Dr. Jill explains, the moment we have a thought, a chemical is released in the brain. It travels throughout our body, and we have a corresponding physiological experience. In other words, if you tell yourself *I am a moron* (or a more colorful version of that), then you are going to feel like somebody rubbed your internal organs with jalapeños. On the flip side, if you think *I am built for greatness,* then you are going to feel like you're in the final two during the last five minutes of a reality show — and this time you *know* you are going to get picked — as the winner!

The physiological sensation you experience as a result of your thought is not permanent. Dr. Jill writes that our physiological experience will last about ninety seconds. After these ninety seconds, we'll have a new thought, and a corresponding new physiological experience. This is great news if we are adept at choosing higher-level thoughts during the many moments when we identify that our Critics, Cops, and Cheerleaders are producing physiological sensations that are mucking us up. Of course, for most of us, this is as simple as winning the Tour de France without doping. After those first ninety seconds, most of us go right back into the same Critic, Cop, or Cheerleader thinking, again and again, and our physiological responses go on loop.

Think about the last time you got up to present an idea that deeply mattered to you. Undoubtedly you had the thought, *I'm scared.* (There was probably also a dirty adjective on the front or back side of *scared.*) Then your body reacted. Depending on your wiring, your heart rate may have sped up, your knees may have started knocking, or it may have felt like your large intestine swallowed your small intestine. Yum.

Then, when your ninety-second physiological reaction was up, I'm banking you went, *Oh, [insert your name]. You're [insert the thought that triggers the same physiological response].* This pattern continued, endlessly, like a mockingbird calling out for its mate through the night and into the dawn. As a result, when you finally did speak, you were a hot mess. More specifically, you were in your head rather than in your body, the words you used may have been coherent but it's unlikely they were particularly compelling, and you almost definitely failed to foster genuine connection with the person or people you were striving to make a positive impact on. You (we all) need an intervention — one you both create *and* execute. In other words, it's not okay to do what I've been guilty of doing (what most of us have been guilty of doing), which is to read about a new behavior or strategy, say to yourself, *Woah, that sounds ah-ma-zing,* and then not do a darn thing about it.

This intervention I'm about to share with you works. It's simple. And really, like any habit that takes a bit of time to create (approximately twenty-one days if it's a brand-spankin'-new habit and ninety to 120 days if it's a habit that is replacing an existing habit, which this is), it simply requires a commitment to consistently practice it. And this new habit I'm asking you to create, your self-talk intervention, is inviting in the Coach to talk back, disrupt, and ultimately change the tone of the communication in your head. I promise, this isn't woo — or high theory. It's incredibly practical, and it works.

The voice of your new soul sister and friend, the Coach, is curious. She asks you questions that empower you to see opportunities amid obstacles. This part is massively important, so let me repeat it again.

Your Coach always asks questions.

Sometimes, lots of questions. This empowers you to turn your inner monologues into dialogues, rewrite your mental script, and prompt feelings that support your most high-powered speaking. Your Coach, she is a great conversationalist. The more face time you give her, the more you will reclaim your role of protagonist in the narrative running in your head. Through this process, you'll also be set up to address the source of your unproductive self-talk. Fear. A lack of worthiness. A nagging in-law. (FYI: I have very supportive in-laws, fortunately, but I've heard some stories.) Simultaneously, you will boost your self-confidence. And as a result, the way you feel in your body and how you communicate in it.

I want to be very clear. While I want your thoughts to create feelings that lead you to be a confident and competent speaker,

I am *not* telling you that you aren't entitled to all your feelings, including the gross ones. When somebody constantly interrupts or belittles you, or you experience a devastating loss — a divorce, a death, a dance party gone wrong — punch your pillow, ugly-cry your way through a box of good chocolate, and hug everyone on your contact list who will let you. The only way through what you're feeling is — wait for it — through what you're feeling. What I want, as it pertains to your communication, is for you to liberate yourself from the unpredictable moment-to-moment physiological responses your self-talk is producing, particularly when it comes to high-stakes communication. Then and only then will speaking be something you look forward to doing, something you do well, and something that produces the results you want for yourself and others.

So how do you translate all this into practice? In real time? How do you let your Coach talk back to your Critic, Cop, or Cheerleader? Well, for example, if you find yourself being in the audience of your Critic, you might be saying: *I don't have the credentials to apply for the director position in my department.*

When you invite the Coach in, she asks: *What results have you achieved in your current role, and how do these make you uniquely qualified to fill this new role?*

If the voice you wrestle with the most is the Cop's, she may poke at you with something like: *You can stay in a j-o-b that you enjoy as much as a colonoscopy — or you can quit, move into your parents' guestroom, and try the whole entrepreneurship thing. What's it going to be?* (Disclaimer: About two years into my business, and two years into my marriage, my husband, Steve, and I moved cross-country and lived in my parents' guestroom for two years. We saved heaps of cash, and we bought our first home as a result. If this option sounds like defeat to you, know it actually wasn't so bad for my hubs and me, or for my parents — or so they say.)

Nonetheless, your Coach is bored by the narrow worldview of your Cop. Even if shacking up with family is what you ultimately decide to do, your Coach wants you to explore other options before settling on a decision. Therefore, she responds by asking, *What are possible third, fourth, and even fifth scenarios I can consider? (Quit and take on some freelance jobs while building my business. Ask to go half-time in my current role so I can take on private clients two days a week.)* It's equally important that you invite your Coach in to pull your Cheerleader out of the clouds and back down into reality. Consider this self-talk messaging.

It's fine that you are hosting a big retreat during a weekend when both your husband (co-parent) and mother (backup childcare) are out of town. A toddler would make a fun playmate for a dozen women who've made a big financial investment to work with you. Yucko. If your Cheerleader is anything like mine, she can be as snarky as she can be sweet. In this case, you could (I did) deal with your equal parts crappy situation (and in my case, delusional impulse solution) by asking: *Who are the people constantly offering to watch your daughter, and how can you send out an SOS and ask for some much-needed childcare coverage?*

I hope it goes without saying (but I like to dot my i's and cross my t's, so I'll risk being what my uncle used to affectionately call me from time to time, an oracle of the obvious, and make it clear) — when your Coach enters the conversation and asks a question (and sometimes she may ask a few questions), you answer them. No, this doesn't make you ripe for a psych evaluation. It means you are laying the foundation for stepping into your moxie — by empowering your communication from the inside out. You allow yourself to dialogue with yourself, as long as is necessary, until your Critic, Cop, or Cheerleader retreats and your Coach is left alone to host the show in your head.

POWER UP YOUR INNER COACH

Directions: As you've read this chapter, you've likely realized that your Critic, Cop, and/or Cheerleader has had a lot to say to you over the years. In your journal (or, if you prefer, you can download a worksheet at AlexiaVernon.com/MoxieBook), identify the message that most often appears in your head when you find yourself thinking about stepping into your moxie. Then identify whether it's coming from your Critic, Cop, or Cheerleader.

Example

Message: Lex, you are a sorceress of suck, and you have nothing of value to offer the world.

Whose Voice? The Critic

Then identify the question your Coach can ask when this voice starts to speak. The question should be short, easy to remember, and able to fast-track you back to being in your moxie.

Example

Coach's Question

• What's a moment of personal awesomeness I can remind myself of?

Now it's your turn!
Not sure what your Coach can say to reset your power in the

moment and, ultimately, long-term? Here are a few of my favorite Coach questions, by category.

Favorite Coach Questions

FOR CRITICS

- What's a more accurate depiction of myself?
- What would I say if [insert name of loved one] talked about him- or herself this way?
- When have I been resilient in the past?

FOR COPS

- What are other possible options?
- How is my judgment undermining me?
- Who do I need to forgive to set myself free?

FOR CHEERLEADERS

- Who can I ask for help?
- What can I take off my plate?
- How can I adjust my timeline?

QUESTIONS FOR REFLECTION

- What would be the payoff for asking your Coach's question each time the message you identified above pops into your head?
- How is the answer you get when you ask your Coach question not only empowering but also a more accurate reflection of who you are — than what your Critic, Cop, or Cheerleader says?
- How might the voice(s) of your Critics, Cops, and Cheerleaders be a default safety mechanism?
- How is your outer communication evolving as your Coach voice becomes a habit?

Let's chat a bit about this second-to-last Question for Reflection. Our Critics, Cops, and Cheerleaders — yes, they impede our inner and ultimately outer communication success. However, they are also there to protect us, in their own way. Ultimately, we have to make a choice about whether we want their so-called protection.

Whenever we step into our moxie and take strategic risks by speaking up for ourselves (or others), we are declaring to ourselves (first and foremost) that we are built for greatness. That we reject playing small in our lives. Our Critics, Cops, and Cheerleaders — they're testing our resolve. Are we ready to play to our edge and capitalize on our potential? Or do we need an excuse, a.k.a. our self-talk, to stay quiet, underearn, hold on to toxic jobs (or clients), and not realize our dreams?

Yes, choosing to invite the Coach in each and every time a Critic, Cop, or Cheerleader speaks requires consistent practice. But this need not be complicated. It requires less time than a bathroom break. It's a simple choice.

Do you believe that your voice matters?

If your answer is yes (and I'm sure it is, because otherwise, why would you be reading this book?), you will make the commitment. You will invest the time to shift your self-talk and activate your most powerful voice. Sure, en route to putting your Coach on autopilot there will be times when you forget, but your commitment will be resolute. You won't make excuses for your mediocrity. You'll stay focused on the results you want and buff up the communication muscles needed to achieve them.

You'll also develop the ability to unhook from other people's opinions of you. Truly, when you stop using, *What if people don't like me? Or what if my boss/clients/partner/parents/accountant/*

personal chef (a girl can dream!) disagree? as the filter for how and what you choose to communicate, you stop yourself from sculpting encyclopedia-like messages in your head that you never get out into the world. You fall (back) in love with your voice. You stop yourself from speaking diluted, inauthentic versions of what you want to say. You live and speak from your whole body — knowing that what comes out of you is what you are supposed to say. Stepping into your moxie is as much about (okay, actually much more about) surrender as it is about elbow grease. It's also about being flexible, integrating our feminine with our masculine, and allowing our communication to be as mindful as it is magical. In chapter 3 I'll share one of my favorite metaphors for thinking about and activating your most authentic and high-impact communication in the world — so that you can develop a speaking presence as powerful as your self-talk.

CHAPTER *3*

BUNNIES DON'T BELONG HERE (BUT CHEETAHS DO)

I think it's healthy for a person to be nervous. It means that you care — that you work hard and want to give a great performance. You just have to channel that nervous energy into the show.

— BEYONCÉ KNOWLES

I did not want to write this book. Although writing comes naturally to me — so naturally that as a junior in high school I wrote a full-length memoir and less than a year later a graphic novel about a high school girl who lost her virginity (and ultimately her life) on a Greek Orthodox youth trip to the homeland — I know that throwing myself into book writing not only arouses some wonky ideas but in the past has disrupted my productivity, my social life, and my business revenue. But I guess you could say this book chose *me*. During the Christmas holiday of 2016, I vowed I was going to take ten days off from my business, a period of time I had not taken off since the birth of my daughter three years earlier. And during my work break, the vision for this book arose, and the corresponding book proposal just poured out of me.

I figured if a book was going to wake me in the night, the least I could do was to listen and type the words that were flowing from me. By New Year's I was three-fourths of the way through a book proposal I was crazy in love with, and by late winter, I was ready to show my *Step into Your Moxie* book proposal to agents. But after I was rejected by the agent of one of my business besties (or more specifically, told to triple my email subscriber list and then get back to her), I caught a nasty case of the "I'm not readys." I was weighing my publishing options, thinking smaller and smaller with each possibility I brainstormed.

And at the height of this shrinking, one very early morning, while driving to the airport to catch a flight to a college speaking gig, I nearly drove over a bunny that was running across the road. Over the next few days, I saw a lot of bunnies. On chocolates. On trinkets in store windows. In my dreams. This mass emergence of bunnies felt like it could only be signaling one thing — and it wasn't good.

I was performing like a bunny.

Let me back up momentarily.

I have fantasized about a certain literary agency for years. They represented one of my first mentors and many of my favorite authors. Despite the many notes I had scribbled in my journal about my literary potential next steps, whether to even look for an agent or self-publish (or in my low moments, put *Step into Your Moxie* on a bookshelf next to my ridiculous senior-year erotic tragedy *A Prayer beside the Sea*), at no point did I write down, *Send a query letter to your dream literary agency, Lex.* But when I got home from my speaking gig, I woke up the next morning, haunted by all the bunnies, sat my tush down, and sent out that query letter. In about an hour, I had a phone call from the agent I had queried, and by the end of the conversation, an offer for representation. "I want this book," Agent Steve, as he is affectionately referred to in my home, said. "I want to represent *you*."

There is zero chance I would have queried my agent, and as a result, it's very likely you would not be reading this book, if it weren't for the onslaught of bunnies. While bunnies are soft, cute, and cuddly — whether they are in Easter baskets or on the cover of a *Playboy* magazine — as an archetype they unfortunately represent one spectrum of feminine power in my world, and if you stick with me, soon in your world too.

Bunnyitis

When I teach about feminine power and influence, I use the bunny as the image of what we do when we don't speak up for ourselves. When we police our ideas and censor them before they ever get expressed in the world. When we care more about people-pleasing than people-activating. When I saw all the bunnies, I realized they were mirroring back what I was saying to myself. Every day I neglected to send a query letter to my dream literary agency and instead started asking myself, *Who do I think I am to write this book?* (despite the fact that this book was poking at me during my waking and sleeping hours to be written), well, that was quintessential bunny behavior. For when a bunny presents her ideas, she:

Apologizes. Sometimes she does this literally. "I'm so sorry I'm late," "I'm sorry I interrupted," or "I'm sorry that I want you to make eye contact with me before you tell me we are going with your idea rather than mine." Other times, she apologizes metaphorically — by speaking softly, by not taking up space with her body, by using diminishing language like "I just want a sandwich" or "I think I'm ready for a sandwich" — rather than owning, "It's lunchtime. I'm taking a break to eat my green-goddess sandwich."

Overexplains her ideas. She informs rather than persuades, she often repeats herself, and when presenting she hides behind other people's opinions, facts, and statistics rather than arguing on behalf of her own ideas: "The Dalai Lama says the world will be saved by the Western Woman" rather than, "From over a decade of leading women's leadership experiences, I have seen firsthand how women who practice their communication in safe, supportive environments are more likely to step into their moxie at work, at home, and in all spheres of life."

Does not communicate a compelling point of view. Because she is terrified of disrupting the status quo, she does not share her unique perspective, her hopes, or her fears (or repulsions), and as a result is as forgettable as she is lacking in impact.

Fails to call people to action. Whether she is negotiating her salary or trying to make a persuasive case, she will not be direct about what she is asking for — or if she does ask (i.e., for an assistant, for a new client, for a house cleaner), she'll keep talking after she says what she wants, unintentionally communicating that she does not believe she is worthy of what she has asked for.

Dragonosis

On the other side of the feminine power spectrum is the dragon. Dragons are, ahem, fiery. They are the antithesis of the bunny. They are the stereotypes of women who are so disconnected from their feminine power that they are hyper (and almost cartoonish) in their performance of masculinity. Dragons are characters like Meryl Streep's in *The Devil Wears Prada*. Or Sigourney Weaver's in *Working Girl*. (In *Alien* she's pure moxie.) Joan Crawford, in probably every movie she was ever in, qualifies as a dragon. When a dragon presents her ideas, quite unlike the bunny, she:

Makes it her way or the highway. Her words are always about her rather than the people she is speaking to. Her body language is rigid and closed off. If she makes eye contact, it's forced, designed to dominate rather than connect.

Shuts off her emotions, including the good ones. She comes across as cold, in the process not only robbing herself of insecurity and discomfort — or at least the appearance of those feelings — but also cutting off the oxygen supply to feel-good emotions like joy and gratitude.

Speaks and operates like a lone ranger. She has bought into the myth that a powerful woman gets to where she is on her own and doesn't ask for help, doesn't ask for feedback, and doesn't obtain group support to champion her ideas. As a result, when she demands action, she may get initial buy-in — but rarely does that lead to long-term follow-through.

While bunny and dragon communication look incredibly different in action, they are by-products of the same interconnected issues. A habit of contorting oneself into who we think others want us to be — as leaders, employees, business owners, partners, mothers, sisters, and daughters. A fear that dropping the mask we are performing behind will be harder than sustaining the masquerade of excessive likability or toughness. And, ultimately, feeling like we don't have a model for what a better way would look like, we execute clichéd gendered personas. Sometimes, these stereotypes are placed directly on us. In the media and popular culture, rarely do we see images of female influence beyond the bunny or the dragon. And for women of color, of course, the situation is even less rosy. Sure, Shonda Rhimes has given shape and voice to richly complex, multidimensional African American, Latina, and Asian female characters, yet these women are most definitely the exception rather than the norm on television.

When I started seeing all those bunnies as I agonized over what, if anything, to do with the proposal for this book, my inner Coach (almost on autopilot after close to a decade of hanging out with her) asked, *Lex, how are these bunnies a mirror for something going on in your life right now?* With a bit of embarrassment, I realized I was setting out to write a book about stepping into one's moxie and yet, in my own self-talk, I'd completed stepped out of mine.

Harness Your Cheetah

When I was eight years old my parents divorced, and my mom remarried. My stepdad raised me as if I were his own kiddo. And even though he did some strange things that drove both my mom and me bonkers — like arguing that the Holy Spirit was a real person and asking friends and family to punch him in the stomach so they could experience the magic of his rock-solid forty-year-old abs — he also had a beautiful obsession with animals. He daily broke out into Louis Prima's "I Wanna Be Like You" from *The Jungle Book*, and he watched boatloads of Animal Planet shows. I've always been drawn to cats, and through my stepdad, my love of cats extended to other less domesticated felines. I enjoyed leopards, a lot — so much, in fact, that I dressed in a leopard-print dress (and safari hat) for my "personality" speech during the Miss Junior America Pageant. "When you look into the eyes of a leopard, it's like you can see into her soul. So I like to wear leopard print so people can see mine." Yawn. Eye roll.

I also really enjoyed watching cheetahs — on television. Cheetahs and I have yet to meet without a screen between us. Nonetheless, I know cheetahs are pretty badass. They can accelerate faster than any other land animal — up to sixty-five miles per hour in a few seconds. They have flexible spines, which allow them to take big strides when desired. They like to hang out in a place where they have a clear view of their surroundings. And they also rest a lot. Plus, they've got those big, arresting, present eyes (and tear marks) — that run from the inner corners of their eyes down to the outside edges of their mouths.

Unlike the bunny, who demurs, and the dragon, who spews fire, the cheetah has got it going on. To recap, she is fast, flexible, and present; she rests as needed and has tear marks permanently imprinted on her face. From a communication standpoint, when she presents her ideas, a woman who embraces the essence of the cheetah will:

- Ask for what she wants (and deserves).
- Speak *with* (versus *at*) her audience.
- Focus on audience connection (eye contact, humor, and storytelling, as appropriate).
- Be flexible en route to getting what she wants.
- Be present with her emotions — and use them to enhance her persuasiveness.

When she speaks, a cheetah has tremendous presence. However, this presence feels born out of worthiness, not performance. When she stands to speak, her:

- Weight is balanced between both feet, hip-width apart.
- Shoulders are pulled back, and her chest is open.
- Eye contact is real — soft, and also absolute.
- Face is neutral and inviting. (She doesn't worry about smiling because when she is in her moxie, her eyes and mouth naturally do it for her.)
- Hands connect from her heart to the heart(s) of her audience. (She makes gestures with her hands that move her message from her body to those who are listening to her. Whether she is using one hand or both, these gestures

work together with her words to move people to take action.)

- Movement is used to convey a change of thought or draw attention to important ideas. (She walks, and gracefully takes up space, to share her ideas. When she is in the middle of an idea, she is so rock-solid in what she has to say that her feet are rooted in the earth, and she doesn't pace or bounce from one foot to the other.)

When a woman shifts from communicating from bunny or dragon energy into cheetah energy, awesome things unfold — for her, and for the people she is seeking to move through her communication. For a number of years, I ran a nine-month, face-to-face women's leadership program in Las Vegas, where I live. And while the cohorts of women who participated mostly entered the program more as bunnies than dragons, most years at least a couple of women showed up on day one in full-on dragon mode.

Candace, despite being one of the younger participants in the program, was one of these women. During our third session, on public speaking, she came up to the front of the room and gave a very polished speech. There wasn't a filler word in it. She sustained eye contact the entire time she spoke. But after she finished, the energy in the room was heavy. It felt as if she had just run us over with her five-minute persuasive speech — which, truthfully, I can't remember the subject of. Whether it was about why poaching elephants is wrong or why a banana would crush an orange in a wrestling match, it doesn't really matter. The speech was loud and word-perfect, but it also felt angry. Very.

When she finished, I asked Candace, "What's something surprising about yourself that you don't tell most people, for fear it would undermine your credibility?" She answered. Let's pretend she said, "I have a tattoo of a caterpillar encircling my navel." I continued to ask her questions that she didn't have answers rehearsed for and that forced her to be present and in her full body, at times even be a little uncool and raw — and above all, real.

Candace was never a smiler. She always had a look on her face like she had to solve global famine in the next twenty-five minutes to prevent the apocalypse. But from that day forward, she started smiling a lot — and she did it naturally. From a place of power and presence. She started to ask questions rather than seeking to prove her wisdom by professing to have all the answers. With her armor off, she started to make genuine friendships with the other women in the program. And her relationships with her coworkers also strengthened. At our next women's leadership session, Candace shared that the throngs of difficult people she worked with (and was previously complaining about) were no longer so difficult (with the exception of one meanie, because there's always one of those).

Over the next few months, Candace also made some epic waves in her organization. She championed a women's leadership initiative and earned a promotion, complete with new job title and salary. She even spearheaded a service project that she mobilized other women in the program to participate in. When she shed her dragon skin, which was never hers (it's never anyone's), she stepped into, well, her moxie.

 **COMMUNICATION AUDIT**

Whether you default to bunny or dragon or regularly show up and speak from your inner cheetah, there is likely still room for you to amplify your cheetah-like inner and outer communication.

Directions: Take the following quiz to learn how you would communicate in each of the following situations. For each scenario, choose your unconscious, default response: A, B, or C. While I suspect that you know which animal or mythological creature you lean toward, a little introspection can only deepen your self-awareness. Afterward, score yourself, and depending on your results, put into practice my recommendations for befriending (or falling into deeper love with) your cheetah. (If you prefer, you may download a companion worksheet at AlexiaVernon.com /MoxieBook.)

Step into Your Moxie Communication Audit

1. You are sharing a new idea you are passionate about with a client or supervisor, and the person is not making eye contact. You ask:

   A. Is there a different way you would approach what I'm suggesting?
   B. Is my passion making you uncomfortable?
   C. I want to understand how what I'm sharing is landing for you. Is this a good time for us to do that? And if not, when would be better?

2. You are giving a presentation at an industry event. You most likely begin with:

   A. Research or statistics.
   B. What you want your audience to take away from your presentation.
   C. A personal story.

3. A mentor sends an email about a prestigious opportunity she thinks you'd be a great fit for. Your first thought is:

   A. This would be perfect for me in a few years.
   B. I wonder who else in my network is applying for this.

C. How do I create the time and space to complete a stellar application?

4. You disagree vehemently with something a family member just said. In response, you:

A. Keep your lips sealed.
B. Passionately argue your perspective.
C. Ask, "Can you explain how you came to that opinion so I can better understand?"

5. You feel like you are stuck in your current professional role. As a result, you:

A. Start looking for new opportunities online. This is your problem to solve.
B. Do the minimal amount of work that is necessary to get by in your current position, and blame others for your discontent.
C. Ask yourself, What is this frustration here to teach me? And what can I do about it?

6. When you need to communicate information that another person is unlikely to want to hear, you will likely:

A. Send it via email.
B. Use whatever medium is necessary to communicate it quickly — and without emotion. Often this means via text message.
C. Set a day and time to have a face-to-face conversation. If that's not possible, you'll speak to the person on a video call so that you can connect as much as possible.

7. After somebody gives you negative feedback, you often think to yourself:

A. I have so much work to do on myself.
B. That person is a [insert expletive of your choice].

    C. I need some time to process what I just heard and to decide if and how I want to respond.

8. There is an opportunity you are interested in, and the investment is more than you feel comfortable making. You:

    A. Cross it off your wish list and move on.

    B. Take out a new credit card to make it happen. You are unstoppable.

    C. Ask if there is wiggle room with the price or an extended payment plan option. And you ask God/ the universe for a sign. If it's meant to be, you'll get a cosmic wink.

Now total your As, Bs and Cs.

_____ As

_____ Bs

_____ Cs

If you are mainly As, you're the quintessential bunny, honey!

Recommendations: Your biggest opportunity is to reframe fear and discomfort as an opportunity for you to practice speaking your truth and putting your voice into a conversation — and into the world. When you focus on connecting with the person/ people you are speaking with, your self-doubt will diminish. And remember, when you step into your moxie, you give other women (and men) permission to do the same!

If you are mainly Bs, then you are going through life armored up, dragon lady!

Recommendations: While we are always entitled to communicate what's on our mind, is your excessive directness serving you? My hunch is, it probably isn't. Moving forward, how can you prioritize working *with* the people you are seeking to influence versus proving that you are right or seeking to overpower? How might being vulnerable and coachable actually elevate your influence rather than undermine it?

If you are mainly Cs, when you are uncomfortable, you take a step back, assess, and make it about connection (with yourself and others). You are a cheetah!

Recommendations: You are doing so much right in your inner and outer communication. Why are you reading this book? I'm kidding, of course. Even though your home zone is the cheetah, stay mindful of your self-talk. Make sure you are defaulting to your inner Coach. Whenever you are unsure of what to say or how to proceed, pause, take the time you need, and prioritize connection over perfection.

QUESTIONS FOR REFLECTION

- If you consistently communicated as a cheetah, what would that look and feel like?
- What would you be able to do more of? Less of?
- What impact would this have on your connection to your voice, on your confidence, and on the results you achieve for yourself and those you care about?

If you recognize bunny, dragon, or perhaps both tendencies within yourself, which can happen (because remember, both tendencies stem from fear-based self-talk), this is a chapter you'll want to come back to frequently. Study (and practice) my recommendations for cheetah presence. And remember, the way to pivot into your cheetah energy is to make a habit of firing up your inner Coach.

Be curious.

Ask questions.

Find the opportunity within every obstacle.

Speak what is aching to come out of you.

And above all, connect.

While I offer coaching and training programs at a variety of price points, working privately with me isn't cheap. Whenever somebody makes a big investment in me (and in herself) to do so, I always ask *why*. And while I've heard a lot of answers over the years, the most common one has to do with my presence.

Lex, you are real, you are honest, I feel like you really care, and I trust you.

That's what moxie is all about. Confidence, clear and compelling communication, and above all deep, deep connection. With ourselves, so we can show up and connect with the people we are trying to influence with our messages. And, when we are communicating, with the person or people in our audiences. If we are going bunny or dragon, it's because we simply aren't in true connection with others.

In the next chapter, we'll look at one of the most important nuggets of our communication — our words. We will learn how to choose words and phrases that are clear and compelling and that make us credible. And how to recognize and adjust communication behaviors we lasses frequently engage in that undermine our influence so that we stay in our cheetah zone. I'll also share with you my favorite tactic for finding your words in any situation — from a vulnerable, hot flash–producing conversation with a disgruntled client or colleague to a high-profile presentation in front of your judgiest peers.

4

WORDS, WORDS, WORDS

Be sure to taste your words before you spit them out.

— AULIQ ICE

When I was in college, I played the role of a chimpanzee named Milton in David Ives's one-act play *Words, Words, Words*. I hated it. Not being a chimpanzee. I got a real kick out of that, at least initially, until I got the full script and realized that the director had cast me as the realistic, practical chimp — the one who defends authority figures and seeks to curtail dissent. And it thoroughly bummed me out. I mean, if you are going to play an ape, you want to be a little crazy, and promiscuous, and throw your feces around. Am I right? (Maybe not the poop part, but the other stuff.)

In Ives's world, Milton is joined by two other chimpanzees, Kafka and Swift, and they are all caged by a scientist, Dr. Rosenbaum (whom you never see), who believes that if the three chimps sit at typewriters and hit random keys for an infinite amount of time, they will create Shakespeare's *Hamlet*. It's a ridiculous play, clearly, and yet my casting awoke a realization in me. It underscored something I'd been struggling with most of my life: the reality that everyone, even my closest friends (like the director of the play at the time), both saw and heard a different version of me than the version of Alexia I'd created in my head. For in my head, I would have been better cast as Swift, the more ambitious, and ultimately rebellious, of the monkeys. A chimp who waxes poetic, unlike Milton, who in addition to being practical also doles out sarcasm and possesses a perpetual air of annoyance. Or if Swift was too much of a stretch, I fancied I could have been a halfway decent Kafka. The only female of the three chimps, Kafka is quiet. Hopeful. A dreamer.

Since I am a self-anointed wordsmith, the idea that people saw me as pragmatic, disciplined, the upholder of the status quo devastated me. And yet so many people in my life gave me this subtle, and sometimes not so subtle, feedback that they couldn't all be wrong — no matter how much I hoped they were. When I took a step back, I realized that while my words on paper read zany, fantastical, and at turns disruptive, what I said out loud rarely was. The same girl who wrote a teen quasi-religious-erotic novel and almost secretly self-published it her senior year of high school was the same girl who always sided with her teachers and professors rather than commiserating with her friends. She was the girl who could get elected class president or class secretary, but not the class spirit officer. The girl whose passionate fan mail could elicit personalized responses from bestselling authors and senators but who was rejected from three-fourths of the jobs she applied to in high school and college for "not being a culture fit" — code for not fun enough to stand behind the register and sling soft drinks or CDs. I lived a secret life in the plays, short stories, books, and term papers I wrote — one in which I used a voice, vocabulary, and point of view that didn't match how I showed up and communicated in my real, human-facing life.

Then, somewhere in the transition between my college and graduate school years, I changed. The me on the page started showing up to the rest of my life. It started on the stage. I jockeyed for roles in plays that were super outside my comfort zone, playing prostitutes, adulterers, and murderers, where I had permission, and once cast, a responsibility, to use communication I'd previously only used when behind a computer screen. Concurrently, I started dating (and ultimately marrying) a guy whose propensity for dirty jokes and physical comedy gave me the space to bring the parts of myself I cultivated onstage into the rest of my life.

Fast-forward almost two decades, and who I am in one sphere of life is a near carbon copy of who I am in all the others. And one of the most important vehicles for aligning who I am in my writing with who I am with my family, friends, and clients? My words. I choose my words like I choose my fruit. I pick them up. I play with them. I ensure they are ripe (but not too ripe). Firm (but not too hard). And when I speak them, I savor every bite. I choose words that embody my voice and my point of view. This book is not called *Step into Your Confidence*. There's nothing wrong with that book, other than the fact that it's not in my voice. Similarly, if you gave my clients a dollar for every Lexism they could name, you'd definitely be feeding many juice and java habits! From "It's not fear, it's sensation" to "Drop the expert shtick," I speak words and phrases that are uniquely me.

Ideally, the words we speak to ourselves, write on the page, and speak in the world all sound as if they are coming out of the same person. And yet for many of us there is a tremendous disconnect — and not simply between our self-talk and our interpersonal communication. Many of us are deaf to the tone of our own communication. As a result, we wonder why the people in our lives don't see and respond to us the way we think they should.

Several years ago I had a client, Vanessa, let's call her. Vanessa came through one of my digital programs, and then she enrolled in a private coaching program with me. When we first decided to coach together, Vanessa confided that she had recently come through some dark times. Money was lean, and she knew the way she had been functioning as a coach wasn't working for her. Whenever she pitched herself for speaking gigs and coaching opportunities, people showed interest. Once she got them on the phone, it was as if they had ants in their pants and needed to get off as quickly as possible and apply some antihistamine. Or a cold compress. Do something, anything, other than stay on the phone with her. Then she'd follow up, and predictably, given their earlier behavior, she rarely heard back.

Less than a month into our work together, I understood why. Spending an hour with Vanessa was akin to hopping on a red-eye, landing somewhere across the country, heading straight into a day's work, going back to the airport, and taking the last flight of the day back home. You could make a drinking game from counting the times she would say, "Don't take this the wrong way," and then launch into an account of everything that was wrong in her life, in her head, and of course, in our work together. Another one of her choice phrases, "This is not working," showed up in her emails to me at least four or five times a month.

The most tragic part of all this was that Vanessa had no idea she was an energetic vampire — draining her own blood in addition to siphoning off the vitality of those around her. It wasn't until her coach (that would be me) feared the onslaught of another angry email tirade more than losing Vanessa as a client that she (yes, again that's me) brought this all to Vanessa's attention. I knew that who I was seeing, reading, and hearing was not the real Vanessa, and fortunately, Vanessa was committed to changing once she realized what she was unknowingly doing. And in mere weeks, Vanessa, and her language, evolved big-time. She gave her all to curbing her anxiety and cynicism, and she created new habits in her thinking and messaging. She started using words and phrases like *thank you* and *this is exciting*. And as a result, she started to get prospective clients onto calls — and closed them.

Now, even after a few wins, Vanessa was as capable of self-sabotage as the rest of us. Her burgeoning opportunity-centered self would be confronted by fear, her old curmudgeonly self would re-emerge, and I'd hear about how everyone in her life, including me, was so horrible we all would surely lose a Nobel Peace Prize to a dictator. Or, at the very least, to someone who wakes sleeping babies. But for the most part Vanessa did evolve. Her new cosmic-wink-oriented, more free-spirited self showed up in the world — through her words and energy. And not only did this shift positively impact her business, but it also built trust and deepened connection between her and everyone in her family.

Cure the Bunnyitis

As women we often spend several hours curating what we are going to wear before a job interview, an important client meeting, or an appearance onstage. Now, I think what we wear matters big-time. Our clothing choices say volumes, encyclopedia cases (remember those?), about how we think about ourselves. Our clothing provides context, and when not done right, disruption, to the ideas we speak and argue on behalf of. Yet I'm also making an impassioned plea that we put as much energy into choosing our words. In chapter 1 we discussed how the way we narrate stories about who we are, what we've been through, and our potential to get to where we know we must go next is the foundation of moxie. Our inner communication births our outer communication. In addition to being deliberate about our stories, we must get even more granular. We must clear the clutter — from our closets, sure, and also from the communication we put into the world through our thoughts, stories, conversations, and presentations. To step into the fullest expression of your moxie, you need to address these linguistic bunny habits that can diminish your impact — even when you think you are communicating with a positive mindset. Here are some of the most important bunny habits to conquer.

Making Unnecessary "I Think," "I Feel," "I Believe," "I Mean" Statements

Whenever you open your mouth to speak, it's inferred that what you are about to say is what you think, feel, believe, or mean. Yet women will often plug the word *I*, followed by one of these verbs, at the start of an idea they are sharing. When we do this, we send the message, "What I'm saying is untested. I might be wrong. And whether or not I am, don't take what I'm saying too seriously. I'm swimming in self-doubt."

Using Too Many Adjectives and Adverbs

In school I did really well on standardized tests in the sections where I paired synonyms. I can still give you at least five different ways to say that something looks nice without taking my fingers off the keyboard. (classy, elegant, pleasing, graceful, stylish, chic, fashionable). I couldn't stop at five! Most women are similarly adept at describing people, feelings, situations, and so forth with descriptive words. Real influence, though, comes from *showing* our own and others' qualities in action. For example, rather than saying, "I'm a hard worker," show how you identified a solution to a problem your team presented you with. "I reduced our expenses by 20 percent and increased our net revenue by 30 percent." When we overuse adjectives and adverbs, it often signals that we are choosing ineffective verbs. Which leads me to the third bad-bunny habit.

Overusing Weak Verbs

We make poor verb choices several ways. Often we use passive verbs. We consistently make statements like, "I am working hard in my career" instead of, "I secured twice as many contracts for my company than projected." Or we say, "She is a great speaker" rather than, "Her words elicit trust and commitment." Other times, we fail to select verbs that convey our unique point of view. Did she "walk into the room" or did she "saunter"? Are you "find-ing your voice" or are you "reclaiming, and shouting from the rooftop, your point of view"? Strong verb choices empower our communication.

Trying — Instead of Getting It Done

In the 1984 movie *The Karate Kid*, Mr. Miyagi muses about com-mitment: "Daniel-san...either you karate do, yes, or karate do, no. You karate do, guess so [as he makes a squishing gesture] just like grape." When we use words like *maybe, hopefully*, and *proba-bly* instead of saying, "Yes, I'll clean the toilets before your parents arrive" or, "No, I don't do toilets, let's hire a cleaning service," we undermine (or to be consistent with the image, squash) our power.

Qualifying

Providing context is great when we want someone to see some-thing, particularly if it is novel or unorthodox, from our vantage point. "Because I broke my tailbone two times (true story!), I have a unique lens on what does and does not constitute a comfortable plane seat." However, when our context lands more as a disclaimer, for example, "I don't have a lot of experience in X area, but I was thinking…" then we minimize ourselves and our ideas. Using the word *but* is one of the most common ways we qualify. I used to proselytize that the word *but* was the most useless word in the English language, but that might have been more dramatic than accurate. Sometimes the word is necessary — as in the previous sentence. Many times, it isn't. Usually we use *but* because we want to provide a bunch of context, protect ourselves, and be polite before saying what we really want to say. "I wish I could get you that report early as requested, but I have a lot on my plate and I'm still waiting on information from a third party before I can complete it." In instances like this, we, and the people who are listening to us, would be better served if we came out and said: "Unfortunately, I don't have what I need to come in ahead of the deadline."

Pitching Up

In high school glee club, I unsuccessfully passed myself off as a soprano (so I could stand and sing with all my friends), when I was actually an alto. The director didn't know what I was up to, but I missed so many notes that he encouraged me to step out of the choir as a singer and choreograph instead. I accepted, and I had the great pleasure of turning all my friends into vaudeville dancers for our Yankee Doodle–inspired musical review. Not reaching the high notes embarrassed me in high school (even though I wound up with an unexpected and fun opportunity to choreograph as a result). However, my deeper voice has served me well as a speaker and leader. As women we often go too high at the end of our sentences, when, in fact, research shows that our ideas land more credibly when our voices lower at the end of a sentence. When our voice gets higher, as it does when we are asking a question, we suggest that we are unsure of ourselves and our ideas. Let questions be questions, and statements be statements.

Asking Unnecessary, Approval-Seeking Questions

Remember that time I told you to let questions be questions? Well, not all questions get a green light. When you find yourself about to ask a question because you are seeking approval or validation, skip it. Examples of this include questions like, "Do you agree? What do you think? Want to give it a try?" Instead, share what you think, feel, believe, and mean (without saying *think, feel, believe*, and *mean*). "Our country needs more female CEOs." Or "Butternut squash ravioli followed by a tiramisu and Italian coffee is the…Best. Dinner. On. Earth." And, thanks to your modeling, other people will likely tell you what they think and feel too.

Mistaking Verbosity for Influence

My junior-year high school English teacher changed my life — many times. She taught me the power of a well-placed comma. (*Let's eat Grandma.* I mean — *Let's eat, Grandma.*) She also reined in my rambling after marking a year's worth of essays with the words *Be succinct.* A compelling, concise statement can move people to action more than protecting ourselves by hiding what we want to say underneath too many words.

Using "Sorry" When You Are Anything But

The chief way to go bunny is by saying "I'm sorry" — and usually, it's when we have no reason to be. "I'm sorry, I actually asked for the dressing on the side." "I'm sorry, I didn't get that email." "I'm sorry, I have something to say, dang it, gimme some face time!" We might say *I'm sorry* because we feel as if we have inconvenienced

(or are about to inconvenience) someone — when we are assert-
ing ourselves. Sometimes we say "I'm sorry" because it feels like
the polite thing to do. Other times we do it because, knowingly
or not, we are actually hoping for others to take responsibility for
their mistakes. We can also say "I'm sorry" with words like *just*: "I
just need five minutes of your time" or "I just thought of a question." (I contemplated putting the tendency to overuse *just* in its
own category, but because it's really another way of apologizing
for saying or asking for what we want, I parked it here.) Certainly
there are times when an "I'm sorry" is warranted. And during
these times, we have an opportunity and responsibility to say how
we have learned from our mistake and how we will self-correct
moving forward. Cleaning up messes is sexy; so is stepping into
one's moxie.

Evacuate Dragon Land as Well

A couple of years ago I weighed the pros and cons of supporting
a hotshot colleague with a project of hers. In addition to determining whether I had interest in her content (which I did), and
the time to dedicate to the promotion (which was more question-
able), I also needed to suss out whether or not the opportunity,
and the person behind it, would appeal to my audience. In the
end, I passed on the opportunity.

While I did have a lot on my plate, my time (or lack of it)
wasn't the main reason. I passed because I realized this person,
despite her brilliance, and despite her notoriety, isn't somebody
who projects a lot of warmth. She comes across as a bit of a
dragon. And this wasn't conjecture; I'd experienced her fire firsthand. And as a result, despite this colleague's wisdom, I felt gross
about promoting her to my audience.

During the only face-to-face interaction I had with her, years
earlier and before she had a massive platform and hundreds of

thousands of people following her, she told me that one of my ideas was naive. And although she'd known me for less than two minutes when she delivered her assessment, I walked away from the conversation feeling like she had gobbled my self-esteem down in the green smoothie she was drinking. In hindsight, I now know I *allowed* her to usurp my power — both in the way I had communicated with her and in the importance I'd placed on her impression of me. Nonetheless, it took me several months to regain my footing and pursue my idea for my Step into Your Moxie platform.

It's easy to see warmth as something subjective or innate. And certainly some people bust out of the womb more prewired for warmth than others. While one overarching moxie goal is to liberate ourselves from our bunny tendencies, again, we also must ensure that we don't step into the dragon realm. And one of the fastest ways into dragonland is through words and phrases that make the people we are speaking to feel unappreciated, unworthy, or unsafe. Here are some dragon tendencies I encourage you to slay.

Name-Calling and Idea-Bashing

I have a hunch you know you're in the dragon zone when you call someone a wench or a loser, or tell someone her idea is lamer than a Ford Pinto. (I mean, really, how did Ford release a car and not know how easily it would explode — and that when it did, the doors would jam shut, causing drivers to burn to death?) While we probably don't succumb to obvious name-calling and idea-bashing often, when we feel unseen, undervalued, or threatened, we often do use subtler fighting words. And sometimes we don't even know we are doing it. "You didn't give me what I asked for." "My last assistant never asked so many questions." "That idea would never work." Sometimes the less obvious jabs hurt others even more — for their subtlety makes it harder for the recipients to call us out for them.

Asking Angry Rhetorical Questions

"What's wrong with you?" "Did you think I'd be okay with that?" "Do you want me to yell at you and call you a moron?" When you ask a question that is not really a question but rather an exclamation point at the end of personal affront, you are doing the dragon dance. As every parent on every children's show advises, take a breath. Count to four before you say anything else. And strive not to be so dragony in the future.

Saying "I'm Fine" When You're Not

The problem with saying we are *fine*, and the reason this point landed in dragon territory rather than bunny, is that we often say we're *fine* when we are not, and when we are actually seething inside. Trade in this passive-aggressive lie for a true, compassionate description of how you are feeling. "I'm disappointed that you passed off my idea for a laundry-folding robot as your own in today's meeting." Then make a direct request for how that person can help. "In future meetings, I'd appreciate it if you would credit team member ideas and contributions."

Using Violent Phrases

Let's blow it up.
You better bang this out tonight.
I'm going to crush you (even with a cartoonish accent).

Violent phrases abound in everyday speech. And while they might make us feel powerful, ultimately they undermine positive influence. (I learned this the hard way when an advertiser removed an ad I posted that had the words *twisted the arm* in it. The full sentence I wrote was "I twisted the arm of an event organizer to get a speaking opportunity." Now, I did send a lot of pitches, but no physical contact occurred.) Sometimes our violent language is barely audible, whispered just loudly enough for someone to hear it. And in these instances, usually our intention is to be nasty. We mumble something passive-aggressive (or in my case, when I'm overworked and skimping on sleep) aggressive-aggressive. "You're such a bonehead." Good idea to omit these snarky utterances too.

STOP AND SMILE

To step into the fullest expression of your moxie, it's vital to ditch words and phrases that sabotage your influence. We've explored some of the chief offenders in this chapter. Many of these ineffectual words also emerge as vocalized thinking, or as filler words, which we speak when we are not exactly sure what to say next. I'm referring to words and phrases like *um, so, like, okay, anyway(s)*, and *you know*. We use them when our brains and mouths fall out of step, and we need a moment to realign. These are some of the most damaging words to our own (and others') perception of our moxie, and fortunately, some of the easiest to weed out. Enter the practice of Stop and Smile. When you Stop and Smile, you literally stop what you are saying, even if it's midsentence. And you smile, and breathe, and make eye contact with whomever you are speaking to (rather than concede to the temptation to double-check that the sky is still blue or that your shoes are scuff-free). Whether you Stop and Smile for a millisecond or for half a minute, you resist the temptation to vocalize your thinking with an *um, so, like, okay, anyway(s),* or *you know,* and prioritize connection over verbal communication.

Directions: Identify your go-to filler word (or phrase) that you use when you need a moment to think and collect your thoughts when you speak. Not sure of your crutch word or phrase? Ask somebody in your personal or professional life whom you trust and are open to receiving feedback from. Then make a point, every time you feel that word/phrase poking its way through your lips, to Stop and Smile. (I want you to know that at the start of my speaking career, I was addicted to the word *um.* I can't watch old presentations without feeling like I'm going to choke from embarrassment because I must have said *um* at least once for every minute I spoke. After a thirty-day commitment to Stop and Smile several years ago, I have almost entirely eradicated the habit.) You can do this!

QUESTIONS FOR REFLECTION

- What is your go-to filler word (or phrase), and when do you most use it?
- As you make a new habit to Stop and Smile, what do you notice about your vocalized thinking (or lack thereof)?
- How does knowing that you can Stop and Smile any time you are unsure of what to say embolden you to assert yourself more?

The first time I launched an online program, somebody I liked and considered myself a mentor to was so inspired by my vision for a coming-soon page that she went to my web designer and had her create the exact same template for her — substituting only her program facts and biographical details. Fortunately, I stepped into my moxie and compassionately addressed the situation with both of them. A little over a year later, though, a similar situation unfolded. This time, however, it was with another speaking coach. She took the name of one of my events, gobs of messaging from my free trainings and sales emails, and used them in her own marketing. Stealing from other people, in any way, is a violent act. And while people can, and likely will, steal your words or ideas from time to time, they can never take your power and perspective, your "secret sauce," unless you let them.

Finding, or more accurately, (re)claiming our voice, and showing up and speaking out in the world with power and authenticity is a head, heart, and gut process. In our first four chapters together, we've explored how to think and feel our way into our moxie. In the next chapter we'll explore the role of our gut. From how to discern her rumblings to taking action on them, even when it's wildly inconvenient (which it often will be), it's time to make some space for the woo.

CHAPTER 5

YOUR GUT AS YOUR GUIDE

*When you reach the end of what you should know, you will be at
the beginning of what you should sense.*

— KAHLIL GIBRAN

I love my clients. I really do. It's painful for me not to give them
my cell phone number or call them at the crack of dawn when
I've woken up with an idea for one of their presentations. I've
never subscribed to the belief that work and life are separate. If
I don't want to take a client on a family vacation, I don't want to
coach her — or him. (The men who aren't scared off by the fact
that they comprise such a small fraction of my client population,
who raise their hands and say, "I need to step into my moxie too!"
— I adore them.) Which is why, if I don't get that *I just devoured a
delicious dessert* feeling after talking to a prospective client, I pass
— except for this one time.

A few years back, at a time when I thought I'd be a bit more flush with cash than I was, someone reached out to me, saying she wanted to work together. A friend of a friend of a friend had said I was the person to help her become more motivational (and less instructional) with her speaking. Although this person, let's call her Gwen, didn't say anything wrong during our discovery phone call together, I not only didn't get the gooey dessert feeling, but I instead got super itchy, almost as if I had hives, while we spoke. I couldn't wait to hop off our call and take a shower. Later in the day, when I typed out an email with enrollment details for the coaching package she had expressed interest in, my stomach and throat burned as if I'd just swallowed a jalapeño pepper, and I secretly hoped I'd never hear from her again. There was no rational reason, yet, to *not* want to work with this beautiful, successful woman — beyond what my body was doing to me every time I thought about her.

Three weeks later I received confirmation that Gwen had signed up to work with me. After we had two or three coaching calls together, Gwen learned she had been invited to give a prestigious speech for an organization I was affiliated with. She wanted to know if she could come for two days and work with me in person. This was a big deal, given that I live in Las Vegas and she lives on another continent. During our first few virtual sessions, Gwen and I spent a lot of time talking through her childhood issues — which left her distrusting women (her analysis, not mine) and chronically courting others' (particularly senior men's) approval. Every time I tried to bring up anything related to speech coaching, the thing she'd hired me for, she said, "I just need you to tell me what to say and how to say it — you are so good at what you do, and I want to speak just like you." The investment I presented to Gwen for us to work together for an additional two full, in-person days was substantial, so I was elated when she said, "I'm booking my ticket and flying out to you in two weeks."

The two days Gwen and I spent together were as enjoyable as the time I was five years old and got stuck with my claustrophobic grandmother in the elevator of her apartment building for an afternoon. From Gwen coming down day one with an upper-respiratory infection and asking to work from her bed — where she writhed around, moaned, and hacked away while I tried to patch together her disjointed ideas into something resembling a speech — to discovering the next day that the speech Gwen had "downloaded" in the middle of the night she had literally downloaded from somebody else's TED Talk, I couldn't wait until the clock struck 5:00 PM on the second day of our work together and I could peace out. When Gwen emailed, once she had arrived back home several days later, saying she finally felt ready to really tackle this important presentation that was now only a few weeks away, and asked if she could purchase some more time together, I told her, without reservation, "No, you cannot."

I felt awful that Gwen still did not have a finished presentation after our time together. I felt awful that I didn't use the word *plagiarism* in reference to what Gwen was attempting to do with somebody else's speech. I also felt awful that whether Gwen was chastising me for not accommodating her desire to work around her body's clock (and beginning our days at five o'clock each morning) or deriding the service staff at the hotel where she was staying for not meeting her lengthy list of needs more quickly, I swallowed my ire and did not speak up for myself, or in the case of hotel employees, others. And I felt even more awful that I had ignored my body's deep knowing that this was not going to be a good client relationship simply because it was financially convenient for me to do so.

One of my favorite teachers once said, in reference to the idea of listening to your gut, that if you listen to what it wants it will give you indigestion. I respectfully disagree. Intuition is the ability to know beyond experience and facts alone. Indigestion comes when we don't listen to or take action on what we are seeing, feeling, or experiencing. Whether our intuition speaks to us via the feeling of a baby going for his or her black belt in utero, signaling from deep within *don't do it*, or a series of coincidences or even a déjà vu–like vision, telling us, *Heck yes, it's your time*, our intuitive hits are one of our greatest guides for what to say and how to take action. My intuition has spoken to me in a variety of ways throughout my life. Sometimes it feels like the branch of a tree blowing in the wind, tickling my arm as if to say, *Pay attention to the thought you are having right now — it's an important one.* Other times it's been the emergence of an idea, seemingly out of nowhere. For example, *Lex, you should start upgrading to first class* — and then a day later I receive an email from my airline telling me for the first time ever that I've earned enough points to receive a first-class upgrade.

How to Call In Your Intuition

I never thought about my intuition as a vehicle for guiding my communication and behavior until one of my first coaches showed me, and a group of fellow coaches, how to muscle-test decisions we were struggling to make. In a seminar she was leading, my coach demonstrated the body's power to tell us what is best for us. She asked for a volunteer to hold something, a sugar drink packet (the kind you would pour into water), and to put it in his dominant hand. Then the man was instructed to hold his arm straight out, at shoulder height, the packet balled up in his fist. My coach told the man to keep his arm straight up and out as she applied some pressure on it. And as she gently pushed on his arm, it came shooting down to his side. He could not, despite being a big guy, hold his arm in the air. Then my coach replaced what the man was holding with a packet of green tea. She provided no commentary on what she was giving him; she simply did a quick swap of packets. The man held the new packet in the same fist, put his arm up in the air, and this time, even as my coach pushed considerably harder, the man's arm did not move.

In less than a minute, this guy had gone from Gumby to Popeye. It was incredible. Afterward, my coach explained what she had done, the difference between the two packets, and how the body had little to no resistance when the man was holding something very unhealthy for him, and conversely, tremendous resistance when holding something healthy. She encouraged us to similarly test ideas, questions, and opportunities we wanted an intuitive response to. And I have, for almost a decade since. From mundane questions like, "Do I get a pedi before my vacation or on it?" to more significant ones like, "Should I take the next six months to develop this idea I can't shake into a new group program?" I ask my husband, a colleague, or a friend to exert pressure on my arm as I muscle-test any decision I don't feel I can make based solely on evidence, past experience, or desire — which is most decisions.

Similarly, I've invested time, study, and observation into getting clear on how my intuition speaks to me in real time so that when my intuition is in direct opposition to what the rational decision might be, I don't chicken out of listening to it, à la what I did with Gwen. I've always been pretty adept at noticing positive intuitive hits that signal I'm on the right path. *Come on, little Lex, your pot of gold is up ahead.* It's been a bit trickier to know when my intuition is signaling that something is off purpose or off path, versus an opportunity to harness my moxie and confront a short-term challenge (and therefore growth opportunity). Like telling a client I don't think we're a good fit (which I now have no problem doing) or pulling the plug on one of my favorite leadership programs — because while I love the curriculum and the women in it, I just know it has run its course.

The key has been cultivating my capacity for intuitive discernment, by which I mean the ability to differentiate an intuitive hit telling me *not* to do something from fear or resistance that is emerging because something is unfamiliar, consequently scary, or might elicit pushback (but is nonetheless the right thing to do). The good news is that the distinction is quite obvious if we know what to look for. When fear or resistance emerges, you may feel it in your body via constriction or waves of worry and anxiety that you cannot surf over and through, and you also feel it big-time in your head. Your self-talk goes Negative Nadine. And as you mentally toss around your options for how to proceed, not only do you get all meanie-pants on yourself as you play out what might happen if you do proceed, but you also realize you would likely nail an audition for the role of Sociopath on an episode of your favorite legal drama. Because the chitchat going on in your head is objectively as nutty as a bag of trail mix. When your intuition is speaking a big fat, hairy, greasy *no* to you, the experience is actually quite different. It's peaceful. You *know* you mean *no*. Any of the other yucky, messy feelings that come up — they come from thinking about how to follow through on taking action on that *no* and not from the *no* itself.

How Does Your Intuition Speak to You?

In my early days as a communication and leadership coach, I was hesitant to talk to my organizational clients about intuition. I figured they would write it and me off as too New Agey or woo-woo. But a number of years back, when I received a long-term consulting contract to design and deliver experiential communication and leadership training to new nurses who were transitioning from the classroom into a hospital setting, I knew I needed to discuss intuition in tandem with teaching how to speak up when it's uncomfortable. Now, nurses are not typically trained to think about, talk about, or, God forbid, use their intuition — particularly if it contradicts their education or training — just as they are not encouraged to go above (or against) doctors or more experienced nurses. At the time, I was reading the book *Crucial Conversations*, and the authors mentioned a study in which they found that, across the world, only one in twelve nurses speaks up when she sees someone, often a doctor, "taking shortcuts, exhibiting incompetence, or breaking rules." Yet if just over 8 percent of nurses (yes, it's so shocking I needed to repeat it) speak up, what rational conclusion could be drawn other than that nurses need training on how to have crucial (or what I prefer to call "daring") conversations?

And here's the tie-in to intuition. As the daughter of a nurse, I know how many times my mom's instinct that something was "off," and her commitment to saying so, saved a life. I felt compelled to illuminate the fact that many of the instances when the nurses might need to step into daring conversations would occur because they intuited that a problem, often medically undetected, might be on the horizon. During our work together the nurses would, as my husband's Hawaiian family would say, "talk story" about the times they had already followed their intuition versus doing what they "were supposed to do." And as the nurses self-reported in our group discussions and evaluations, they found it immensely helpful to now have a vocabulary to describe what they knew but couldn't name or therefore explain.

One nurse talked about telling a charge nurse she "had a hunch" a patient might be adversely reacting to a medication (even though the doctor making rounds said everything looked good) — and she was right. Another shared that she suspected one of her patients was withholding embarrassing (and critical) information about his medical history, and indeed he was. However, these nurses explained that the more experience they gained, the more they found themselves distrusting their intuition when it was out of alignment with what they were supposed to do because it felt "unprofessional" to counteract their past experiences — which should scare any of us who anticipate ever needing hospital care.

Intuition isn't a mindset or skillset that either you have or you don't. We all have it, fortunately, and yet most of us can get a heckuva lot better at both recognizing it and following through on the messages it's sending. And to do so, first it helps to know how you are receiving your intuitive hits. Consider the questions below, and give yourself a *yes* (without overthinking it, please) if what I'm asking occurs for you most of the time. And give yourself a *no* if it typically does not.

A. When you enter a room, are you usually able to identify the attitude of the people in it (kind, curious, eager, disinterested, hostile)?

B. When you meet someone for the first time, is your instinct about whether she or he is trustworthy, and a person of integrity, usually accurate?

C. Do you make life decisions against the advice of experts or loved ones because you feel, deep within, that there is a better answer for you?

D. Do you know that the phone is about to ring just before it does?

E. Do you know who is about to call you, just before they do?

F. Do you just know where a lost item has been hiding?

G. Do you wake up in the morning clear about an answer that, prior to sleeping, had you stuck?

H. Do you have visions of upcoming events (good or bad) before they happen that prove to be accurate?

I. Do you meet the exact person you need to connect with in order to take action on a big idea or project?

J. Do you see signs (images, numbers, words, or patterns) that illuminate what you are supposed to say, how you are supposed to take action, and what, even if it's outside your control, is about to transpire?

Kinesthetic Intuition

If you answered yes to questions A, B, or C, your intuition speaks to you kinesthetically. This means you feel your body's knowing. Maybe, like me, you get a swirly feeling in your stomach. Or you may even feel as if a cat is tickling your chest with its whiskers. Or perhaps you feel a subtle shift in weight — you feel pulled forward when your body is indicating *yes* to an idea or, conversely, you feel your body moving backward when your intuition is signaling, *Stop yourself before you wreck yourself, señorita.*

Cognitive Intuition

If you answered yes to questions D, E, or F, at least one of the ways (for none of these categories has to be mutually exclusive) that you intuit is via cognitive awareness. In other words, you have strong hunches, what I refer to throughout the book as aha moments. You just know things, and you are right about them (whether or not you want to be).

Experiential Intuition

If you answered yes to questions G, H, I, or J, you experience intuition experientially. You are in the right place at the right time, you see what you are supposed to see in order to know what is coming, and/or you experience coincidences (that likely give you goose bumps) because in hindsight they make so much darn sense!

Intuition Helps You Unhook
from Judgment and Approval

I come from a family of dancers. While my grandma, my mother's mother, only danced in the privacy of her own home, she dreamed of having a daughter who was a ballet dancer, and she got her wish two times. My mother consistently took ballet classes and performed semiprofessionally before she found her true passion, ballroom dancing, in midlife. And my aunt, her sister, was accepted into the New York City Ballet as a teenager (which is the equivalent of a football player being drafted to the NFL in middle school or a gymnast competing in the Olympics in elementary school). After winning accolades from George Balanchine (please don't kill me, Auntie E, for dating you), she went on to dance on Broadway and act in television and film.

Growing up, fortunately, I had the antithesis of a stage mom. In fact, she constantly told me, "Please *do not* make a career of this. I don't want you to destroy your body or be unemployable by the age of thirty." But my genetic predilection for ballet was intense, so by the age of four I asked my mom for ballet lessons. By first grade, I started winning our yearly elementary school talent show. And until I moved to New York and there was no longer any room in them, I frequently danced through supermarket produce aisles, with fruits and vegetables in my hands. As a result, despite not always feeling comfortable opening my mouth to share my opinions, I did feel very comfortable performing, or going into a local Gelson's Market and giving an impromptu performance.

I loved the security of choreography and character. All I had to do was master someone else's steps or words, and I felt as happy and secure as a high school senior with an acceptance letter to her favorite college in hand. I developed a habit of equating my self-worth with how much praise I generated from my dancing, and later, acting. And the older I got, the more this habit grew, with the intensity of a migraine at a rock concert. I started hustling for others' approval through my academic achievement. I must have broken records for the amount of extra credit I routinely did, all the way through graduate school, so that I could permanently book my seat at the top of the class. Early in my career, I would go on to seek approval from more senior leaders in my organization by outworking my peers. Lest you think I'm so self-evolved I'm liberated from these habits, think again. As an entrepreneur, I now have new potentially unattainable standards for measuring my performance if I'm not careful — which, of course, I try to be. As I create and frequently achieve ambitious goals for revenue, email list size, or program enrollment, I have to watch myself so that I don't conflate what I do (or don't do) with who I am.

Whether it's feedback on our looks, academic or work performance, athletic or artistic skills, or parenting or housekeeping, most women have subcontracted the process of feedback out to the other people in our lives. I won't advise you to isolate yourself from others' feedback. I welcome a stranger telling me I've got spinach stuck in my teeth as much as I welcome a team member telling me I'm clinging more tightly to deadlines than a koala clings to a eucalyptus tree. All of us should stay open to feedback so that we can enhance our capacity to step into our moxie. What holds equal value is filtering other people's opinions about you through the lens of your intuition. Not everyone's feedback needs to be acted on or archived and revisited. When I intuitively know that I've written a dynamite newsletter to the people on my email list, somebody can email me back and tell me my ideas on a social issue I'm passionate about are ill advised or dead wrong, and for the most part I'm unshaken. Similarly, when I pour my all into a speech, and someone (or many someones) gives it a thumbs-down on social media or leaves a snarky message like, "Pay inequity isn't real" in the comments, I can bless and release. And when a client emails to tell me she doesn't like the way we've developed a presentation and wants to go in another direction, if I'm in a place of intuitive flow, I usually know that email is coming — and I also have already put together at least a loose plan of action for how we can pivot and get back on track. When we are in sync with our intuition, nothing others say or do derails us because we know whether or not it's accurate, and we minimize giving ourselves feedback that is often more critical than anything others might say to us.

Do you evaluate the feedback others give, or do you accept it as the undisputed truth?

We need to dispute, or at least question, others' truths — particularly when they are about us, or something we're invested in. Imagine if Magellan hadn't questioned whether the Earth was flat. For starters, I might not be on the airplane I'm on right now, shooting death stares at the gentleman in 22E who refuses to cover his mouth when he sneezes. (Please, if you are on an airplane and you have a cold, cover your dang mouth.) Justified rant aside, how can you be open, unattached, and nondefensive when people provide you feedback, even when it's unsolicited? And how can you run it by your intuition to see if and how you want to incorporate it?

I met one of my dearest friends, Josh, while in graduate school at a summer theater intensive. Josh, like me, has a strong point of view (hence the friendship), and spent much of the summer giving ideas to his student director for how to develop the theater piece we were all working on. She would tell him, "Thanks for your idea, Josh. I'm going to put it in my pocket, and I'll come back to it later." While he wanted to slug her at the time, I loved this woman's candor and saw beyond the palpable condescension. She knew she didn't want the feedback. Full stop. Regardless of your current relationship to feedback, the way to let it empower your moxie, when you've decided to take it out of your pocket and consider it, is to keep your intuitive voice strong. Here is one of my favorite ways to do so.

CLEAR THE VOICE OF FEAR
AND LET YOUR INTUITION SPEAK

Directions: Complete this exercise when you can have quiet, peace, and presence. Once you are ready, read the following prompt. Afterward, close your eyes and strive to re-envision what you read. Don't worry if you can't remember every word. Give yourself permission to stay in the visualization as long as you need to, without forcing an answer. Allow whatever wants to come up to come up. (Note: if you prefer to complete this Moxie Moment through an extended guided visualization, which I recommend, you may listen to the audio I've created for you at AlexiaVernon .com/MoxieBook.)

Imagine yourself waking up after a full night of sleep. You are still in bed, nice and cozy under the covers, leisurely watching the sun come through your window. You close your eyes to allow the sun to warm your body and awaken all of you for the day ahead. Then sun floods your body. First, it moves through your toes. Then up your legs, through your pelvis and back. Next, up through your chest, back, and arms. It continues to make its way up through your throat and onto your face. Your whole body is warm and glowing now from the sun. As you sit with all this light, you realize a question is emerging for you. You can't fully make out its shape yet. You know it's an

important question, so you don't rush it. You allow it to present itself
when it is ready.

QUESTIONS FOR REFLECTION

- Did a question present itself to you?
- If so, what might be the purpose of this question?
- Based on how your intuition speaks to you, how can you be on the lookout for other feelings, signs, or coincidences that can help you carry forth what this question illuminates?
- How can you carve out time each day to squash fear-based self-talk and make space for your intuition to speak?

Whether a question that evoked a big lightbulb moment emerged or, more likely, one with the potential to prompt some future discovery (or maybe even a throwaway, chatter-filled question like, "When can I go to the bathroom?") sprang up, I encourage you to use this visualization whenever you are seeking to connect with intuitive guidance. As you give yourself more time to clear your mental clutter, recognize the voice(s) of your intuition, and apply them in your life, I bet you will discover that translating what you want to say into words that feel honest, provide value to others, and advance your ideas and convictions becomes easier and easier. This has certainly been the case for me — and for the powerhouse women I support. By developing your capacity to recognize and act on the voice of your intuition, you set yourself up to inspire connection, trust, and maximum buy-in for your ideas when you speak — and you make it a whole lot easier to feel comfortable opening your mouth in the first place.

I want you to unapologetically speak up and out, and to enjoy opportunities for visibility, whether that's speaking up in meetings, at conferences, or on larger stages. In the next chapter, I'll show you how to construct any form of communication — interpersonal or presentational — so you can take your internal knowing and translate it into outer impact. You will discover a straightforward, easy-to-remember, foolproof way to structure your communication so that your message easily connects with the person or people you want to move to take action.

6

DECLARE YOUR DESIRED DESTINATION

If you don't know where you are going, then you probably won't end up there.

— FORREST GUMP

W hen my now-husband, Steve, asked, "Will you marry me?" I had the answer to his somewhat rhetorical question, but I did not have the answer to what was, in my opinion, a much more important and pressing question: *Who do I want to be by the time I get married?* At the time, I owed more in student loan money than I made in the course of a year. I served as the director of one program and the manager of another (earning one barely full-time salary for my two roles at the same company). I was adjunct teaching at multiple universities and performing with an experimental theater company most weeknights. Between these roles I patched together just enough money to cover my half of rent for a fifth-floor walk-up apartment on the Lower East Side of

Manhattan. And I was the primary breadwinner! Although my life sounded glamorous to my fellow actor friends, who were slinging coffee and working soul-sucking temp jobs, I barely had any time to spend with my new fiancé (who I had convinced to move cross-country to one of the most expensive cities in the world two semesters shy of his college graduation), and I was more bitter than rancid milk that I constantly felt broke despite how many hours I was working.

Within a week after my guy proposed, I had an answer to my question about who I wanted to be by the time of our wedding. I would be a coach — someone in control of her own time and financial future. With my destination clear, I boldly began to work backward from my dreamy vision and identified the major steps I needed to take to translate it into a reality. Enroll clients. Lead sales conversations. Design an offer. Oh, yes, and give notice to my employer and hang out my shingle.

Within forty-eight hours of making my decision to say, "Thanks, but my services are no longer needed here," I scraped together some additional adjunct teaching jobs in order to almost meet the full-time salary I was abandoning, but I was still five figures short of what I wanted to be earning to feel comfortable leaving my j-o-b and awesome health care coverage while I built my coaching business and new life. I decided that I needed to give notice — and convince my soon-to-be-former employer that they should retain me as a consultant to continue leading one of my projects. From home. And give me a part-time assistant to do it. It was a brazen vision for a girl who thought she could build a thriving coaching business charging her first clients a hundred dollars a month for three forty-five-minute one-on-one coaching sessions. *I can't believe I just confessed that.*

The weekend before I planned to give notice, sort of, I headed to St. Thomas in the Virgin Islands to lead a training for educators that I'd snagged for myself. Seriously, my life wasn't glamorous. Okay, maybe a little glamorous. But I had high hopes that with some more Benjamins, it could be even grander!

I worked my resignation pitch every spare moment I had while I was away. And there were, fortunately, quite a few of them. I practiced my words on the airplane. While walking around my hotel room. Strolling on the beach. Swimming in the ocean. And in less than two days, the thought of making my case in front of an audience not composed of sea turtles no longer made me shaky.

When I returned to work the following Monday, I immediately learned that more than half the employees across departments in my position had been laid off due to one of our big grants not being renewed. And I — still had a job. The survivor's guilt, on top of my already profound stomach somersaults, which returned the moment I exited the elevator and walked into the office, made me seriously question my plan. I sat before my two supervisors debating what to do. They transitioned from telling me that all my friends were leaving in two weeks into how delighted they were with the way I was leading my programs. They assured me that my job was secure. I, however, was considerably less so.

Nonetheless, I decided to stick to my plan and fortunately, muscle memory kicked right in. I nailed my opening story and every beat that followed. I took a quick breath in between my explanation of why I was leaving my current full-time role and beginning my consulting proposal. By the end of my persuasive case, even though I was told I wouldn't receive an answer until many senior leaders had weighed in on my bold, unorthodox request (that was not so keenly timed), I knew that my two supervisors (who had likely fought for me to keep my job) were not only *not* angry with my decision, but they also saw what I was proposing through my rainbow-colored goggles. A few weeks later I officially landed my first five-figure organizational client — my own company.

Begin with the End in Mind

Whether it's a speech, a salary negotiation, a sales presentation, or a request to quit a job and immediately be rehired as a consultant, most of us devise our communication the same way — from the beginning to the end. Spoiler alert: this is the wrong way! Despite what Maria sings in *The Sound of Music*, when you "start at the very beginning," it's *not* always "a very good place to start." Because often you go down a path that does not lead you to your destination. Therefore, I recommend that you always, always, always start with your call to action.

What do you want the person or people listening to you to *do* with the information you share?

And then, work backward from that final point all the way to the beginning to ensure that each thing you say, or ask, is leading you to that precious end point.

Had I composed my words to my employer based on what I wanted to say first, I likely would have said something like, "I'm here to let you know that I'm giving you my two-week notice." Then I would have told my supervisors how much I appreciated the opportunities I had while I worked for our company, yada yada yada. And had I gone down that path, I can all but guarantee that I would not have stayed on as a work-from-home consultant for the next three years, until I transitioned my project over to my friend, Josh, who is still running the project. Also, I did not start off by mentioning the part about primarily working from home. Why? Because had I spoken those words it would have sounded like my idea was about me rather than about *them* — my company. And it would have been.

Instead, when I got clear on my desired outcome, to be retained as a consultant, I concluded that one of the most important things I needed to communicate was my next-level vision for the project I had been running and how the project could serve more educators and young people in our community. And how our organization could increase its revenue as a result. I used this information as a filter for everything I said. I asked myself, *Will what I'm saying help my supervisors see my vision, and make them want to go to bat for me again because of what my ideas could mean for our bottom line and our community legacy?* I reverse-engineered everything I said from my final point, which was this.

"I want to ensure that my vision for this project gets executed. And without me, given that I've been leading this project without a team, I know that it won't. And that would be a travesty. Would you be willing to explore what it would look like for me to stay on as a consultant to produce this project, and allocate a part-time assistant to ensure that moving forward I'm not the only one who knows how to manage all the moving pieces of what we do?"

As I continued to work backward, I discovered each thing I needed to say next. In conjunction with making my case for continuing the project, I needed to present my argument for why I was uniquely poised to be the one to scale it — because my experience and contacts equipped me to recruit more schools and better brand the work that we did to attract more recognition. (Up until that point, I had not been the one recruiting schools, only leading the programming.) During this part of my persuasive case, I needed to be planting seeds about how my recent training as a coach gave me a unique ability to reinvigorate our approach to teacher education and align it more with our organization's mission.

As I reverse-engineered again, I saw that before making my proposal, I needed to transition pretty quickly from why I was leaving my full-time position into how aligned my new work would be with what was needed to advance my project. And as I kept moving farther and farther back, ultimately to my first words, I was constantly asking myself, *What do I need to say (or ask) in order to move my supervisors to the place where they will want me to stay on?* This is why I did not begin by saying some version of "I quit" but rather:

"Through your mentorship, I've grown into a great educator, theater artist, and also dynamite coach. And in order to do more of this work that is my calling in the world, and less administration, which is not the work I feel is my zone of genius, I've made the decision to transition in the next ninety days."

Yes, I gave ninety days' notice (which was super risky) because — as I would go on to explain — I knew how much time and effort my supervisors had invested in me, and I wanted to be around so that I could similarly set up the next person in my role for success. To do so I needed time to clearly map out all my job responsibilities and deliverables and create a robust onboarding plan. As I presented my case, I used stories to show my points versus simply telling my supervisors what I thought, or what I wanted. And I asked questions to keep the focus on my supervisors. Their hopes. Their fears.

"What would make this transition as seamless as possible for you and for our organization?"

"How can I ensure that my replacement is set up for long-term success?"

"What would be the payoff to you, and to our organization, if we were able to double the enrollees in our professional development program while only incrementally increasing our costs?"

This last point created the opening for me to frame my consulting fee as an investment rather than as a personnel expense.

When you begin with the end in mind, you not only set yourself up to have your greatest impact, but you also give yourself a way to manage the sensation you are likely experiencing in your body as you prepare to make your pitch. It's easy to feel as if bedbugs are mating in your abdomen when you decide, *Yes, I'm going to make a bold request and express a potentially unpopular but necessary opinion. But that pain is far less than the pain of swallowing my voice and potential.* And that's saying something, given how violent bedbug mating rituals are. (I'm guessing you did not know that female bedbugs lack a genital opening and the male has to ram his lady's abdomen with his genitals to lodge his sperm in her abdominal cavity. I'll give you a moment to digest that.)

So, to sum up, when you reverse-engineer, you give yourself the gift of channeling all the physiological and mental war games into something productive, mindfully sculpting what you want to say. Rather than ruminating on all that can go wrong, you set yourself up for what can go right.

From Persuasive Communication to Effective Presentations

The process of reverse-engineering also works brilliantly for speeches. When I work with my speaking clients, I have them first identify their call to action for their audiences. Whether they want their audience to change their opinions about a piece of legislation or make a sizable investment in their coaching program, when they know their final destination, and how everything they are saying leads an audience to it, they heighten their impact. Redirecting the spotlight away from ourselves and onto the people we are seeking to influence, and what we want for them, absolves us from having to be show ponies when we present our ideas.

But, oh, do I get pushback on this.

"Lex, can I please open with my joke about the priest, rabbi, and zookeeper who walk into a bar?"

"Lex, I think I should start with this story about the time I survived an attack of flesh-eating bacteria. When I talk about how my daughter provided the blood for the transfusion that saved my life, it always brings on the waterworks."

While I love a good joke or medical survival story as much as the next gal, too many speakers (and communicators) equate being entertaining (or harrowing) with having influence. If your goal is to have impact with your words, don't string together a bunch of anecdotes; instead, curate your content and words to serve your end goal.

Let's imagine you are giving a speech. It could be about something pedestrian, like how to make your bed. Scratch that. My bed-making skills are pretty unremarkable, so let's go with brushing your teeth. (I've never had a cavity, and I'm almost forty years young, so I feel comfortable holding up my teeth-brushing process as a pearly-white example of what to do.) If I don't reverse-engineer, I probably jump right in with talking about why teeth brushing is important. Then I talk about how much toothpaste to put on a toothbrush, how long to brush for, and how to rinse. Whatever my exact words, I do a lot of informing, I probably come across as preachy, and I do very little persuading. I don't change minds. I don't change behavior. And when I end, I do it with something like, "So go brush your teeth." As a result, I have as much impact as dry cleaning does on an ink stain on a pair of yoga pants, which is to say, none.

If I start by identifying my call to action, things proceed differently — and better. First off, I realize that "go brush your teeth" is not very compelling unless my audience consists of preschoolers, so I take a different approach. My new call to action: "kick poor dental hygiene to the curb with a simple (and significant shift) in how you brush your teeth." My call to action could have been "follow my three-step tooth-brushing plan to remove coffee stains." Or "apply my three ways to brush your teeth when you have a screaming, writhing baby in one arm." But we'll go with the first angle. If that's my call to action, then I ask myself:

What does my audience need to hear from me right before (in this case) my final call to action? And how is this leading them toward the call to action?

Let's say my answer is, *A reminder of the payoff of healthy teeth. Fewer mouth bacteria, less gross teeth staining, and more morning sex (I mean, fresher breath). My summary reminds my audience of the payoff for taking action on my main idea — the need to make one pivotal tooth-brushing shift.*

I then ask myself, *What does my audience need to hear from me before that?*

My answer: *I want to tell a story that shows both the privilege of clean teeth and the cost of poor oral hygiene. So before I recap the final payoff, I'll wind down my presentation with a story about a homeless man, whom I'll call Peter, whom I had the opportunity to volunteer with. In our conversations, Peter shared that while he missed having his own home, he missed access to proper oral hygiene even more. Peter shared that as a result of not brushing his teeth, he had lost many of them. And without his teeth, he felt like he had lost his dignity. As I tell this story, I will share my discovery that while brushing my teeth is something my privilege allows me to take for granted, like having clean water or matching closet hangers, through my interactions with Peter I discovered what a privilege it truly is to have clean, healthy teeth — one I must never take for granted again.*

I would, just as in a conversation, continue this process of reverse-engineering my speech all the way back to the beginning. Picking up from my volunteer story, immediately before that I decide to talk about how my shift positively affects the smell of my breath, teeth staining, and bacteria. Before that I want to introduce my one simple shift, and before that each of the common mistakes in teeth brushing. And I keep doing this all the way back to my opening, ensuring that everything I say connects to the idea that comes after it. As I evaluate everything I am devising, I simultaneously make sure that everything is persuasive. That it's leading to my call to action. By using this process, when something feels off in my reasoning, I will know it — because I will see that there's a logic gap or that one or more ideas isn't leading to my desired destination.

REVERSE-ENGINEER YOUR COMMUNICATION

To transfer this process from a concept into a practice, it's time to try it out on some important communication of your own. Whether you are ready to enroll a coworker in your big idea for your department before you present it to your boss, or you want to practice your words for an important sales presentation, find both your reasoning and your words by beginning with the end in mind — and then work backward to your start.

Directions: As I've demonstrated in this chapter, the first part of this process is to establish your call to action. What specifically do you want your audience to think, feel, and above all do as a result of what you have shared? Then reverse-engineer everything you are going to say (or ask) until you work your way back to the beginning.

Use the following two filter questions for each thing you intend to communicate:

- What does my audience need to hear from me right before?
- And how is this leading them toward my call to action?

Write, type, or audio-record your responses to this exercise. (If you want a blank worksheet to complete this exercise, you may download one at AlexiaVernon.com/MoxieBook.)

QUESTIONS FOR REFLECTION

- How was the experience of reverse-engineering your communication?
- What, if anything, surprised you about how to move your audience to take action using this approach?
- What will be the likely impact of reverse-engineering all your communication with respect to your influence and self-confidence?

See (and Feel) the Promised Land

While in this chapter I've provided you with an effective framework you can use to sculpt any form of communication, the equally important piece of moving listeners to take action is giving yourself permission to believe (and the universe the permission to hear your faith) in it. To receive your unwavering belief that it's conspiring on your behalf. In addition to mindfully finding your words backward, similarly envision those in your audience taking action on your ideas. Assuming the best possible outcome will not jinx you. That kind of thinking is malarkey. It's been said by many wise souls that what we see we create, and it's true. While I could write an entire follow-up book solely of examples of this from my own life, I'll give you just one.

Less than three days after I wrote my quip earlier in the chapter about bedbugs, I was convinced I had them in my home. Now,

I live in Las Vegas where people in the burbs, particularly when it's 116 degrees outside, don't usually get these disgusting creatures. Yet my husband woke up during a vacation with bedbug bites all over his body, and when we got home from the hotel, bites continued to pop up on him. Even after a bedbug company came out to our house and gave the "all clear," for months afterward I remained suspicious, more times than I care to admit stripping sheets from the bed in the middle of the night and examining the mattress like a forensic scientist examines a crime scene. Through it all, it was pretty hard not to think the half hour I spent working my joke a day before the first bedbug bites showed up hadn't been the trigger.

So, to recap, you should not joke about bedbugs and other outcomes you really, really, really don't want to experience. Instead, you want to give yourself time and space to visualize what the scene will look like, and how you anticipate it will feel, when people act on your words. Also, please see your audience, regardless of its size, getting there *with* you. See them benefiting from your ideas, not feeling like they got run over by a Caterpillar (the construction vehicle, not the insect). And as we continue to talk about persuasion in the next chapter, I'll share with you bunches of my favorite hacks for eliciting buy-in for your ideas — even if you've spent most of your life, up until this point, swallowing your desires or crossing your fingers and toes in the fleeting moments right before you make a request.

CHAPTER 7

GO FOR THE HOLY YES

Thaw with her gentle persuasion is more powerful than Thor
with his hammer. The one melts, the other breaks into pieces.

— HENRY DAVID THOREAU

M y dad is one of those guys (and while I could say people, the truth is this inclination shows up in many more men than women), who could convince you to invest in landscape maintenance even if you lived in a high-rise. Whether he was selling vacuums, insurance, tires, or warranties on alternators, my dad has never struggled with asking for business — and getting it. I've always admired his persuasive abilities. After my parents divorced, I would visit my dad on weekends and holiday breaks. During the summer, when he had to work during my stays (and my dad, bless him, did not believe in using babysitters during our limited times together), he would bring me along on his sales calls. While he used to joke with the men he was meeting with that I was his secretary — and he would instruct me to take profuse notes — as a youngin', I was more like his apprentice. I soaked up everything he did — how he built relationships with both assistants and decision makers, how he told stories, how he asked for what he wanted, and how he made deals come to fruition — even if they seemed unattainable. Even though I struggled big-time with consistently stepping into my moxie during the first quarter of my life, one of the first areas where I felt moxieful was in negotiating. One of the reasons, and there were many, that I felt uneasy about giving notice to the company I worked for and transitioning into entrepreneurship was that it was with this employer that I first deployed, and quickly buffed up, my negotiation muscles. Even though I was still underearning when I gave notice, I was underearning slightly less than when I had started at the company, and that felt delicious.

I didn't have a grand plan pulled together the first time I decided to ask for a promotion. One day, a few years in, after I felt particularly strapped financially (I realized I wanted to go on a vacation and didn't want Steve to take out more student loan money for us to do it), I talked to my supervisor about why I deserved a promotion. My role had morphed. I had new responsibilities. A lot of new responsibilities. And when I casually brought this up, my supervisor said that while I made a compelling case, she regretted that she was not in a position to offer me a new job title or pay raise. And in response, I harnessed moxie I didn't know I possessed at the time, and asked, "Who is?"

With my supervisor's blessing, a week later I negotiated with our organization's vice president of finance for what would be two promotions, accompanied by two corresponding pay increases, over the next two years. Each time I received almost exactly what I asked for. In hindsight, I now know this means that I wasn't asking for enough! But given that approximately 20 percent of women will never negotiate for *anything*, according to Linda Babcock and Sara Laschever (in one of my favorite books on women and negotiation, *Women Don't Ask*), the fact that in my early twenties I was negotiating my salary, in a nonprofit culture, no less, deserves to be celebrated.

Shortly after the vacation Steve and I were now able to take, to New England (where I fulfilled my dream of doing a Transcendental-era tour — think Walden Pond and Nathaniel Hawthorne's house), I received an after-hours visit from a woman in my company's fiscal office. Let's call her Daisy. Daisy had been at our company for about a year, and she shared that she was a recent immigrant. I'd also learn during our impromptu meeting that because her degree was from a foreign university, it wasn't recognized by our company. And therefore she was making only a hair more than minimum wage. Because she processed payroll, she knew I'd received two promotions in two years — which apparently was unheard of in my primarily female office — and she wanted me to help her negotiate.

Since my work entailed leading participatory professional-development programs, I role-played with Daisy in preparation for her upcoming performance review. I wanted her to find her words — and develop the confidence to use them. I played the role of the vice president of finance, and I was tough. I said no, a lot, forcing Daisy to keep strengthening her persuasive case. Finally, after a few evenings of rehearsal, Daisy went in for her review. The evening after her meeting, she returned to my office, where I usually worked late (because in my last negotiation I had included a request to adjust my schedule so I could start teaching women's studies and public speaking at local universities), and she shared her news.

"I got a no."

It's been a lot of years since that disappointing day, but I know for sure I was more crushed than Daisy. I tried not to let my head go to ugly places — thinking that if only Daisy where younger, or whiter, maybe she would have received a different response. (But in case you can't tell, my head definitely *did* go there.) Several months passed. During that time, word got out that I was running a covert negotiation salon out of my office. Through practicing with me, many of my colleagues got what they asked for during their negotiations, or close to it. And one afternoon, Daisy popped back into my office with a big grin on her face. "Alexia, I got another job. And I'm going to be making more than you!"

It turns out that Daisy's takeaway from her first real-time attempt at negotiation wasn't a *no* but a *not yet*. She had decided, unbeknownst to me, to start applying for the kinds of positions she would have been qualified for in her native country, and another local university did not have the same policies in place regarding college degrees, so she was scooped up. Moxie is most definitely a muscle, and Daisy buffed hers up. And you can too!

The Feminine Reframe

In the 1992 film *Glengarry Glen Ross* (based on David Mamet's play by the same name), the character Blake, played to perfection by Alec Baldwin, goes on a tirade in front of a group of real estate agents, as he passionately tries to motivate them to sell more. Sell harder. Sell better. Amid his profanity and sexist language, he flips over a blackboard that has the phrase *Always Be Closing* on it. He then repeats the phrase several times — drilling into his men that they should always be pushing their customers toward the sale. Unfortunately, this smarmy image of sales that *Glengarry* showcases is what keeps too many women from stepping into their moxie when it comes to money and asking for what they want — for it's the image so many of us have internalized as the norm.

Chester Karrass, a renowned negotiation expert, has authored several books, including *In Business As in Life — You Don't Get What You Deserve, You Get What You Negotiate.* Indeed. When we ask for something we want, be it a company-sponsored coach or the opportunity to be hired as someone's coach, we are not only literally asking for something; we are also announcing through a bullhorn to the universe, and everybody in our lives who can feel the shift in our energy, *I am someone who is worthy of things.* Money. Responsibility. Freedom. An aromatherapy hot-stone massage. We get to choose the energy we wrap our persuasive cases in. It doesn't have to be all testosterone-y. A lot of women haven't gotten this memo, which makes sense, because most of the images of selling we see reflected in popular culture, in the media, and in our institutions reflect masculine values — even when women are doing the selling.

I've witnessed too many women across the age, race, class, and sector spectrum nurse a deep-seated, often unrecognized fear that asking for what they want will unseat the sense of likability they have cultivated for themselves. They would rather remain perpetual bunnies than risk reassignment to the dragon realm. How do I know? When I coach my clients and ask questions like, "What's the worst-case scenario if you spoke up? Made that request? Asked for the sale?" I almost always hear some version of the same response: "I'd be seen as a bitch." The fear of losing a job (or a top client) is the exception (in thought and in reality) rather than the norm. I gotta say, whenever I see these reflections of who I was for so many years mirrored back to me, it feels like someone is taking a scalpel to my aorta — which is only incrementally less painful than when I drained all the oxygen from my body each time I swallowed one of my desires. It's time to emancipate ourselves from our fear of selling by letting the masculine "Always Be Closing" be a footnote in 1990s pop cultural history. Instead, we need a new refrain, one that empowers us to speak up for ourselves and others. To choose grace over force. Collaboration over bulldozing. I propose: *Go for the Holy Yes.*

Yes.

When we strip off the masculine stereotypes of selling that most women, as well as men, have been socialized to normalize (greed, entitlement, being a loudmouth, not taking no for an answer, and at times, outright deceit), and free up space to sell and move people to take action with feminine energy, it really can be a holy experience. And by holy, I'm going to the Greek origins of the word *hagios*, which means "different," "set apart," or "sacred."

"Sacred selling?" I can hear you repeating to yourself, eyebrows creeping up onto your forehead, nausea perhaps rising from your belly to your throat. When we present our ideas in a way that aligns with our values, that treats the people we want to influence with respect (and that respects their right to say no), and that reflects what we feel is in service of their highest good, we are using our moxie for holy work. I'm grateful I grew up watching my dad procure business from a more feminine paradigm. It's one of the key reasons, even in my silent "I wish I could disappear" years, I knew that an alternative model for selling and negotiating was possible — because I'd experienced it firsthand.

So, without further ado, here are some actionable ways for all of us to shift from the masculine paradigm embodied in "Always Be Closing" to a more feminine one, epitomized by "Go for the Holy Yes."

Always Be Closing	*Go for the Holy Yes*
Prove your expertise.	Show your commonality.
Tell people what they want to hear.	Tell people the truth... *always.*

Focus on profit.	Focus on pleasure.
Hold the mic.	Share the mic.
Demonstrate confidence.	Demonstrate kindness.
Show the risk of not acting.	Show the payoff for taking action.
Focus on individual benefit.	Focus on collective benefit.
Send a deli platter.	Send a gift that shows you truly see the other.

Okay, let me explain that last one. While my dad mostly embodied the "Go for the Holy Yes" list, one "Always Be Closing" style move he did make was send deli platters. No matter the situation, if I were to ask my dad how to court a prospective client, or thank an existing one, he would tell me, "Lex, send a deli platter." The problem with the deli-platter strategy is, well, not everyone wants a deli platter. *Sorry, Dad!* While deli platters usually worked well for my dad in the eighties and nineties, when he was calling on a lot of white, middle-aged men just like him, holy sales requires that we see the people we are seeking to move as individuals — with their own set of fears, desires, and gifting likes. So while I don't think I've ever sent a deli platter (although if I ever had a client like my dad, I would get my pastrami on), I have sent hundreds of personalized gifts — everything from fancy-schmancy blenders, to gourmet dog biscuits baskets, to birthstone wishing balls.

A Crash Course in Holy Selling

Putting "Go for the Holy Yes" into action — whether you are speaking, writing, or doing a combo of the two — begins with mindset. And it's supported by "heartset," what you make space to feel. (And speaking of feelings, don't worry; we'll spend most of the next chapter talking about how to manage all the "feels" that come up when you step into your moxie.) Ultimately, it's enacted through a series of practices. Let's take a peek at them so that you can start speaking up and securing creative, purposeful, and potentially lucrative opportunities for your company and/or yourself, right now.

Create Community through Your Words

Peer pressure or groupthink can be dangerous, but it can also be stellar for this feminine and holy approach to sales. When people feel as if they are a part of a community of other people who think, feel, behave, and from time to time self-sabotage like them, they are more apt to listen and take action. And when we can use our words to show that we too have, let's say, struggled (or outright stumbled), and yet have managed to dust off our bums and stand up again, it makes us all the more convincing and trustworthy. We put this theory into practice when we engage in necessary truth telling. We tell stories from our past — that show our not-so-social-media-shiny moments — and the lessons we've learned from them. We use phrases such as, *If you are anything like me, you have [insert something that stings a bit to share]*, allowing your audience to realize that you are as adorably ridiculous as they are. Other effective phrases that create community, and therefore influence, include: *You are in good company if...* and, an equally choice pick, *If we could time-travel back, we would stop ourselves from _____, but of course we can't.*

Speak What People Are Thinking

One of my favorite persuasive hacks is to articulate the potential objections going on for people who are considering something you have proposed — and then to counter said resistance with an equal helping of compelling reason and charm. For example, if you believe someone is thinking, *I can't afford that*, you may counter with: "You're probably thinking about the cost, but really, what I'm proposing is an investment. I'd love for you to move from a scarcity mindset, of constantly cutting costs, into a growth-oriented one. That's what my Super Awesome Program will teach you how to do." Or if you presume someone is thinking, *I don't have enough time*, you shift their thinking with, "I know you feel busy, overscheduled, tired, maybe even a little frantic. So if you don't make a change now, then how are you going to feel a year from now?"

Mirror Back What Has Been Said — and Not Said

When people hear back the words they are saying, it can unlock big-time discovery for them and for you. And when people hear what they are communicating beyond the actual words, it can be equally as revelatory. To use mirroring effectively when you go for the holy yes, you might tell someone who is talking about the importance of innovation, "I can tell being a renegade is really important to you." And if someone is saying she is ready for change but every time the subject of money comes up she grimaces, you could say, "While you're saying you're ready for change, each time we talk about investing in your future, you look deeply uncomfortable. Why do you think that is?"

Demonstrate the Payoff with Your Questions

When you encounter pushback, real or perceived, it's easy to go bunny. "Thank you for your consideration. I'm going to stop talking now and go take a permanent vacation in Antarctica." Then you archive this experience as evidence that you should never go for the holy yes again. In reality, you didn't go for the holy yes. You allowed yourself to be complicit in someone else's fear. To go for the holy yes in such a situation means asking juicy questions that allow people to articulate what might be possible if they say yes. Here are some of my favorite questions for doing this. Adjust them, please, to serve your purposes.

- How committed to resolving this are you?
- What do you really want?
- What lies on the other side of your fear?
- What's your role in this situation?
- Where can you grant yourself some grace?
- Whose approval are you seeking?
- What would be possible with additional support?
- What are you not telling me that would be helpful for us to talk about?
- Why does this really matter to you?

In their book *Yes!: 50 Scientifically Proven Ways to Be Persuasive*, authors Noah Goldstein, Steve J. Martin, and Robert Cialdini make many recommendations that support the practice of going for the hoy yes, including getting people to say "because," followed by the reason they would do something. The last question I proposed above works swimmingly for eliciting a "because" and prompts the person you are speaking with to provide a compelling reason for moving forward. "Because I know I am ready for an effing-awesome everything!"

Put Pleasure before Pain

A central premise of most sales theory and training is that people need to be reminded of the pain of their circumstances to do something about it. I don't know about you, but when I'm in pain, the last thing I think about doing is something new, or different, or bold. Yes, I want to stop the pain. But usually I'll do it the simplest, least creative way possible. Think Band-Aid or anti-itch cream. When we go for the holy yes, we remind people that the outcome(s) we are proposing can create more pleasure in their lives. Pleasure could be having a potluck with friends, decluttering an office, or watching your child lie in the dirt while she stares up at the clouds — as long as it didn't rain earlier in the day. (Because cleaning mud out of kiddo hair is definitely not pleasurable for me.) More time, more money, more freedom, more self-care, more self-worth — yes, yes, yes!

Create Time-Sensitivity If Fast Action Can Benefit Your Audience

If we know that something we are offering or proposing can truly benefit someone, we actually serve their interests more when we provide incentive for them to make a decision efficiently, versus taking their sweet old time (and as a result, breaking up with the desire they finally [re]connected to). Often when someone chooses to change, to grow, to pursue short-term discomfort to facilitate long-term satisfaction, if she doesn't raise her hand and declare she is taking action or moving forward, she will soon revert back into her cozy, fear-based habits and fail to follow through. When you ask people to make a decision, give them a reasonable deadline that allows them to do the necessary critical thinking — but don't provide so much time that it makes it too easy for them to talk themselves out of it or be influenced by others.

Integrate the Masculine with the Feminine...the Right Way

While society has labeled logical, evidence-based reasoning as masculine and more emotional, story-based persuasion as feminine, I've often seen men gravitate toward (and possess more comfort with) telling stories in their persuasive cases than women. And on the flip side, I've seen a lot of women hide behind facts, figures, and research and as a result do more informing than persuading when they present their ideas. Going for the holy yes requires head and heart, and a commitment not to overeducate, overspeak, and underpersuade.

Use Your Chi for Good

You likely have encountered the Chinese word *chi* before, but in case you haven't, its literal meaning is "air" or "breath." When you are making a persuasive case, remember to give yourself time to breathe so you don't race through your words, and to give those you seek to move to action time to breathe and stay in step with your reasoning. Because *chi* can also mean "energy," another way to use your chi for good en route to your holy yes is to bring a mindset, a heartset, and the energy of optimism to how you present your ideas. People want to say yes to those who make them feel good. Use your chi to uplift, to create possibilities, and to show people that what they want can be theirs.

Believe That Yes Is Your Birthright

This is one area where "Always Be Closing" and "Go for the Holy Yes" are in full alignment. Yes: it is your birthright! When you make a persuasive case, ask with the certainty that you are a woman the universe is winking in approval to. You deserve an awesome professional life, an awesome family life, awesome relationships, awesome everything. When one or more areas are not so awesome, take responsibility for getting yourself reoriented toward awesomeness by asking for what you need. And remember, as my former coworker Daisy learned, that when you don't receive a yes now, another yes awaits you, as long as you go after it.

A Lesson from a "Not Yes Yet" Moment

My relationship to selling radically reset after I made my first big offer at a retreat. If you are not in the fields of self-improvement or online marketing, you likely have no idea what I mean by "offer." Here's the deal — pun intended. Coaches who offer high-level (code for lots of Benjamins) individual and group programs will often, at the end of a business presentation, workshop, or retreat, present a time-sensitive opportunity for audience members to work with them. While in hindsight I realize that throughout my years as a coach I'd invited audience members to work with me at various points after speaking gigs, I felt a ton of tummy butterflies leading up to this offer because it was the first time I was inviting individuals (versus organizations) to pay me many thousands of dollars for my services. After the women at my retreat had already paid me a couple thousand dollars to attend. I also wasn't hiding behind my computer, crafting a proposal, as I did with my corporate clients, where I could rely on good grammar and painstaking persuasive wordsmithing to generate my yeses. I had one shot with a live offer — and I was determined to nail it.

During the time of this retreat offer, fortunately I had a deep awareness and appreciation of my skills. I had crossed six figures in my business. A few months earlier I had made my own five-figure investment to join a mastermind and work with a business coach, so I felt comfortable about asking other women to make a big investment in me, since I had done the same for myself. But the idea of standing in front of a dozen women, which included my business coach, and inviting them to join a group program with me — oh, my stars, it felt like my insides were whirling around in a blender.

When it was time to deliver the offer at my event, I felt completely connected to the women in the room. We had just talked about how to use speaking to funnel audience members into coaching programs, so I gave myself a pretty easy opening. I talked about the intense emotion you can feel when you make offers (which helped me turn my internal blender speed from high to a 3 or 4 on the variable setting). I then talked about my own discomfort with offers, and how I used to cringe when I'd hear other thought leaders present them, regardless of how classy and heart-centered they were, because of my own lack of financial self-confidence and my dysfunctional relationship with earning and spending money. I explained how I had been working on my own money stories, and how recently making a big coaching investment, wink wink to my coach, had enabled me to double my income in a year and step more boldly into the spotlight as a speaker and an entrepreneur.

Then I transitioned from myself to my audience. I mirrored back my perception of where the women in the room were a little over halfway through the retreat, where they could expect to be by the end of the weekend, and the delicious support they might be craving afterward. I presented the financial details for my group program, offered a financial incentive to anybody who enrolled while at the retreat, and disappeared into my bedroom at the house where we were all staying, awaiting word from one of my team members about who was signing up.

Nobody was. Nobody did.

I was the textbook definition of crushed — facedown on my bed, big-time ugly-crying. When I came up for air, I told myself that maybe the women just needed time, and redirected my attention into cleaning up my runny eye makeup and executing a powerful second half of my retreat. During the remainder of the weekend, I allowed myself to receive the generous praise the women were sharing with me about my teaching and coaching style. I kept bungee jumping down from my head back into my heart to be present to the experience I was leading. Nonetheless, by the end of the weekend, not a single woman had enrolled. And yet at least a quarter of the group had said, "Lex, I know I want to work with you more. But I'm not sure a group program and a follow-up retreat are really what I'm looking for."

I got home, took a step back, and looked through the notes I had scribbled after my many private conversations. I was determined to adjust my offer and get it right for these women. It didn't take me long to realize I had been working on the design for a one-on-one mentorship program that incorporated everything the women shared they were seeking, and it was at an even higher price point than my initial retreat offer. Over the next two weeks, I circled back around to everybody who had so much as whispered that she wanted more Lex time, and within a few weeks, I closed beaucoup dollars in private coaching.

If I had stayed stuck on trying to sell the women in the room, and move them into the program I thought would be perfect for them (rather than opening myself up to really hearing what they wanted), I have no doubt that those women would never have continued to work with me. Nor would I still call many of them friends. Nor would I have been able to revisit the original group program I had devised, transition it into a more robust yearlong mastermind, and generate six figures when I launched it for the first time the year after. Or more than double my profit when I relaunched it the year after that!

In one of my women's leadership programs, I used to facilitate a role-play activity in which I stepped into the role of Sheryl Sandberg. My participants were then paired into teams, and each had to collectively pitch their plan to me for how they would lead a community book launch event, should I (Sheryl) decide to use their company to produce my event. The women consistently put together compelling plans. Over the years, some pitched intergenerational lifestyle events. A speaker series with inspirational female leaders. Or a charitable event where for every book purchased, one was donated to a woman living in a homeless shelter. But almost every group made the same mistake — they created the pitch and at no point asked me (Sheryl) what my goals were for the launch. Going for the holy yes necessitates knowing what people really want and keeping that knowing at the forefront of everything you say, ask, or propose.

BEFORE YOU ASK, LISTEN

Directions: Think about something you are ready to ask for, whether it's a new team member, a new client, or the opportunity to leave your kids with a partner or parent so you can run away on a girls' trip. Before you so much as utter a word about what you want, put together a series of questions that allows you to find out what the person (or people) you are seeking to move to action want(s). Try not to ask leading questions. Instead, ask questions from a place of genuine curiosity. Then, and only then, take the time to sculpt your persuasive case, incorporating the answers you discovered.

QUESTIONS FOR REFLECTION

- What did you learn from your prepersuasive case Q&A?
- What, if anything, surprised you?
- How can you go for the holy yes and speak directly to the desires and concerns you unearthed?

When you go for the holy yes by staying present, nimble, and in the feminine, you don't edge out ambition, achievement, or profitability. Often, you amplify it. As I hope you see by now, moxie — be it in sales or any other arena — is not something you either have or you don't. Nor is it something masculine you must reappropriate and feminize. It's in you, even if it may feel latent, and it's cultivated and amplified through everyday acts.

While the process of buffing up our moxie can be deeply uncomfortable, as a lot of personal growth and transformation is, we can condition our bodies to gracefully make space for and hold the sensations we are feeling. I'll talk more about how to do that in the next chapter. For when we can allow body tremors to ride tandem with our desires, we give ourselves permission to speak up (even when we aren't completely sure what will come out of our mouths or what the outcome will be). We archive the message, which gets stored in our brains as well as in our cells and tissues, that the totality of what we are feeling is normal. That all that sensation is simply signaling that we are stepping into our moxie, and that we should keep on stepping — for ourselves and for everyone else who is watching and rooting for our success.

CHAPTER

YOUR SPOTLIGHT IS WAITING

When you're able to be honest with yourself about who you are and finally can present your authentic true self to the world, you feel so much better.

— GUS KENWORTHY

A s I rose from my chair, I could feel sweat pooling in my arm-pits, and I couldn't shake the feeling that maybe the noro-virus was setting in. A part of me definitely wished that it was. Then I'd have a reason to run out of the room, puke my brains out, and receive (versus be required to pen) apology notes from my coworkers.

Tasked with addressing the room on something simple and mundane (which of our instructors would be attending the new student mixer or what I was putting in the budget for dry-erase markers), I began with, "Welcome."

I felt and heard *it* immediately. That dang (and frighteningly familiar) quaver in my voice. I tried to put my attention equally on suppressing my desire to cry and on reviewing everything I had ever learned in my public-speaking classes:

Speak directly to each person in the room.

Take a deep breath between sentences.

Use your hands to bring your message to your audience.

Breathe.

Don't die!

I'm twenty-four years old, speaking at a friggin' staff meeting, I chided myself. *I spoke to thousands of people as a motivational speaker in college. I should have this.*

But I didn't.

While that day at my staff meeting I was truly a hot mess as a presenter, the truth is that the psychic torture I put myself through (that too many of us put ourselves through) was far worse than most of the communication that comes out of our mouths. And when we focus on trying to impress others and prove that we are credible or charismatic, we almost always guarantee that we will get in our own way of communication success. Rest assured, a better way exists.

When we develop the capacity to stand before an audience and allow ourselves to be truly seen, our relationship to our inner and outer voice fundamentally shifts for the better. We also give other people permission to step into *their* spotlight. Our act of moxie can start a chain reaction of positive results by triggering many more acts of moxie. And once we know this, choosing to do anything *but* claim visibility (and use our voice to facilitate positive, at times radical, change) — it's, well, a little selfish. Yes, when you play safe and small, you're not just wasting your divine human capital. You're also standing in the way of other people's learning, growth, and evolution.

I fear I'm getting ahead of myself. Let me rewind a bit. For as you now know, for years I could have medaled in self-sabotage if it were an Olympic sport. And the mental, emotional, and physiological jiujitsu moves I've seen my clients perform on themselves before they get onstage are equally heartbreaking.

When I was a high school senior I had the opportunity to colead my first retreat. I volunteered, despite some intense reservations — you know, the whole *I'm pretty sure I'm going to upchuck* reaction I had during these years whenever I had to get up and speak. The year before, as a junior, I had attended the same retreat. One of my favorite seniors had given a powerful speech during which she shared her harrowing story of surviving a violent sexual assault. Afterward, I could no longer deny the abuse that many in my family had been complicit in, that I had spoken up about and then tried my darndest to wipe from my memory. I also realized that when you tell your stories, you give other people permission to do the same. I hoped telling my story might liberate another young woman to tell hers, so despite the terror I felt, I raised my hand and said I wanted to be a retreat leader the next year.

In addition to leading a small group of juniors through a series of interactive activities during the retreat, I also had the opportunity to deliver a speech on finding God. During my presentation, I planned to speak about the many conversations I had with God through the years as I moved through shame, guilt, and anger — and how I always felt I was being guided out of my inner darkness and back into my light. Now, giving class presentations on current events, countries, and presidents through the years had elicited some pretty intense discomfort. But talking about familial sexual abuse in front of a few dozen fellow upperclasswomen at my school? I was pretty sure that would feel like standing in the middle of Times Square on New Year's Eve in my skivvies. During my presentation, I broke most of my rules for stepping into your moxie. I typed out every word that I spoke. I presented behind a podium — clinging to the binder that held my manuscript like a baby orangutan clings to its mother. (And in case you aren't married to a former biologist like I am, you should know that orangutans literally do not break physical contact with their mothers for approximately the first four months of life.) I'm also pretty sure my chin didn't unstick from my clavicle for the first twenty minutes that I spoke.

But then, as I transitioned from my story into what I wanted for my classmates, it was like God found me. Moved through me. I felt golden light flood into my crown chakra, at the top of my head, and spread through the rest of my body — deepening my breaths, quieting my self-talk, and emboldening my delivery. I wasn't alone in this. Even though I didn't break up with my binder full of notes, for the remaining ten minutes I spoke, I began to look up. I smiled. I allowed my classmates to see me. And, more times than I want to remember, I locked eyes with another girl from my school who I sensed had also experienced sexual abuse and saw herself in my reflection. And I sent her, without adjusting any of my words, all the love and compassion I held in my heart.

And the more love I shared, the more I had to give. When I stopped striving for perfect execution of my words and shifted into loving up on my audience, with every cell of my being, I felt like a renewable-energy plant. The more love I gave, the more love I made. I no longer felt like a hostage to my sensation. And my speaking, despite the serious nature of my material, became, yes, fun.

When I finished my presentation, I knew something magical (and in my opinion, divine) had transpired between my audience and me. I was glad that despite the discomfort I experienced at all stages of this opportunity, I refrained from evicting the butterflies from my belly by bailing on the retreat. As I made my way off the stage, one of my teachers gave me a hug — the kind of reassuring hug you keep feeling, long after it's over. And he spoke words that imprinted on my soul for life: "Alexia, keep telling your story. It will help a lot of people." I suspect my teacher intuited something I couldn't have at that time. And during the moments when resistance emerges, or I hit an upper limit for my success, I think about his prophetic words and soldier on.

It's Not Fear, It's *Sensation*

If you're anything like me, or at least who I used to be, my hunch is that when you are on the cusp of doing (and especially saying) something big, important, and paradigm shifting, you label what you are experiencing in your body as *fear*. I really want you to stop doing that. And here's why.

What you are feeling in these moments — whether it's stomach flu–like gastrointestinal pain, the weight of a bookcase on your shoulders, or a tornado in your larynx, it's your body acknowledging that you are on the cusp of something important. If you mine your life to uncover the moments when you felt like you busted through your own glass ceiling — when you spoke your truth, negotiated your worth, crushed a sales call, or found the words to have a daring conversation — my hunch is you didn't feel like you were on a beach vacation. Rather, you felt like a colony of butterflies had migrated for the winter into your thoracic cavity. This is normal. This is you on the brink of stepping into your moxie. And the last thing you want to do is to shove that sensation back down or create a narrative around it that positions you as a victim or martyr rather than as a protagonist — which is what you are.

This sensation thing happens during (and before) most forms of communication when we feel like the stakes are higher than a skyscraper. When we are tasked with articulating an opinion that people might disagree with. Or when we are unapologetic about maintaining a personal or professional boundary. And if we want to consistently step into our moxie, speak up and out, and do it in a way that moves people to take action, we must learn how to get comfortable being uncomfortable.

That starts with giving ourselves ample opportunities to role-play what we plan to say, so that we're old hat at feeling our sensation and speaking through it by the time we have an audience, whether that's an audience of one or one million, or something in between. Now notice, precious reader, I most definitely did not say *memorize*. Memorizing spawns more sensation. It makes you get stuck in your head. If you have perfectionist tendencies, which I suspect you do, trying to memorize what you want to say flares that perfectionism right up. When you role-play, you say what you intend to say aloud, keep your head and heart focused on your final destination, and choose moment to moment to lead your listeners there. When you role-play, you listen to the beautifully imperfect sound of your own voice and try new ways of messaging an idea or phrasing a question. You remember that you're not a talking head, that your body language (how you move from your toes to your earlobes) impacts your audience as much as if not more than your words. So, when you role-play, you put your body into the mix so it can develop its own muscle memory and your gestures pour out of you like maple syrup when it's go time. And when you role-play, you visualize connecting with your audience as you speak. You do all this over and over again, until you no longer find yourself in your head, searching for words. Because no matter how much sensation you experience, your body (not just your mind) has committed your message to memory, and you can speak it even if you are blindfolded, standing on one leg, and holding an entire hard-boiled egg in your mouth.

Most public-speaking textbooks proselytize that speakers should rehearse for approximately one hour for every minute they plan to speak. I can stand by that — for presentations, as well as for any other high-stakes communication situations. Now, if you've made sensation your lackey, you may be able to get away with less role-play time. But if you're still bowing at the altar of tummy butterflies, girl, get up on your feet and walk and talk what you plan to say some more. Because you know if you're not role-playing, you're spending your time ruminating, so you might as well do something that quells sensation rather than something that gives birth to a litter of worry puppies.

I suspect you've heard a lot of this before. You may even believe it, but you're likely not getting more comfortable — because you aren't doing the work. Amiright? So, the sensation still feels diabolically debilitating. As a result, you're doubling down on trying to dull it rather than playing nicely with it — by yammering on about how scared you are or how hard speaking up is. And we need to talk about why this is, chickadee, and what to do about it.

The communication we do internally and out loud is habit based. And while popular psychology has suggested that it takes twenty-one days to make a new habit, most psychological research shows that it takes much longer to break an existing habit and create a new one — upward of sixty, ninety, and perhaps even two hundred plus days, depending on how deeply entrenched the old habit is. Playing nicely with the sensation that comes up around your communication and actually practicing out loud and with your body what you intend to say (instead of telling yourself "I'm scared, I'm a crap speaker, I deserve to feel like I'm sleeping in a bed of scorpions") definitely falls in the realm of replacing an existing habit. And in order to solidify this new habit, we need new language and new practices to put the theory of playing nicely with sensation into continual practice.

How to Play Nicely with the Butterflies

There will be moments throughout your life when you feel sensation in your body, when you know you are *not* supposed to label what you are experiencing as fear — but you have the same willpower as a shark baited with chum. Your higher self doesn't want to concede to your familiar, self-sabotaging responses, but your lower self is calling the shots. In these moments, the key is to disrupt the unfolding narrative and change your physiological response as quickly as possible. To do so, let your first response to what you are experiencing be *thank you*. Yes, I literally want you to say to yourself, in your head or aloud, *thank you*. For why would you say anything but thank you when you are up to something big? Getting onstage to speak. Presenting a juicy idea at a meeting. Telling a partner that you are all in. Or on your way out.

When you respond to what you experience with gratitude, many gorgeous things happen. For example, gratitude relaxes your body, boosts your optimism, enhances your brain function, makes you less prone to comparison, deepens your emotional connection to others, and heightens your resiliency. In other words, choosing gratitude is not an act of woo. It's about creating the foundation for everything you want and need to be a stellar communicator.

As I shared in chapter 2, Jill Bolte Taylor's research reveals that the moment we have a thought that triggers a feeling, we are going to experience that feeling in our body for ninety seconds. When we choose to speak back to our self-talk and the corresponding feelings, we must hang in there for, well, at least ninety seconds. To ensure we don't kick-start another ninety-second tsunami of resistance, it's vital that in addition to choosing gratitude we also choose to be objective about what we are experiencing. This will keep us in an opportunity-centered mindset and decrease the intensity of our sensation.

When I lead speaker training events and coach participants to develop the mental, physical, and emotional habits for compassionate and compelling communication, I often invite someone who confesses she experiences intense sensation when speaking before a group (or simply thinking about speaking before a group) to come onstage with me. For a couple of minutes, I ask her to look out at her audience, breathe, and mentally say *thank you* as she sends love to everyone she sees. It's an intense experience — for the speaker, for her audience members, and even for me. I follow up by asking the speaker to maintain her audience connection and also be objective and describe for us what she is experiencing. Usually, she will begin by saying something like, "I'm feeling scared" or "I'm feeling nauseous." After all, old habits are hard to replace. Then, with some gentle reminders, she'll drop her unproductive story, slow down her breathing, and be a witness to what is transpiring inside her. "I feel my knees locking. I feel my heart beating quickly." Or, as one woman confessed a week before I wrote this chapter, "I feel gas trying to escape my butt!" By this point, between doing the gratitude work and speaking aloud the objective descriptions of what she feels, the speaker starts to smile, and her initial panicked tears morph into tears of pure joy, for she knows she's bulldozing through the resistance that has felt impenetrable for so long. She has shifted her experience from fear to moxie — and gained the ability to turn down its intensity.

Then I begin to ask her questions she will not have prepared answers for. "Why do you know you have to share your message with an audience? What makes you the perfect messenger for your ideas?" And I advise the speaker that any time she doesn't know what she will say next, which is often, she can simply stop — even if it's midsentence. And she can smile, with her eyes and her mouth. Any answer she needs will always be found in the eyes of the people she is speaking with.

When our reason for communicating is greater than our sensation, we will stay committed to figuring out how to say what we want — and this will make it easy, or at least considerably less painstaking, to put in the time to rehearse our communication. And when we remember, no matter what we are saying or where we are saying it, that at any moment if we lose our place we can simply Stop and Smile, allowing our mouths to catch up with our brains, then our worry that if we lose our words we'll never find them again melts away.

The unconscious belief that we are not enough is behind most of the terror we create for ourselves around our communication. And the fool's game in all this is that communication is never about us. Or at least, it is not supposed to be. It should always be about our connection to the people listening to us. At any moment when you are speaking and you lose your way, when you feel the urge to hop on a hot-air balloon and travel from below the neck up into your head (guaranteeing you'll sever whatever precious connection you have created with your audience), all you need to do is Stop and Smile. Connect more with your audience, whether it's with one person or a large group. Allow yourself to be seen a little bit more.

While Stop and Smile did not become a part of my vocabulary and teaching until nearly a decade after I began my speaking career, I accidentally gave myself moments of this powerful practice before it became an unconscious habit. For example, while sharing my sexual abuse story at my high school retreat. Or talking about preventing campus sexual assault during that long-ago pageant. During the rare moments, early in my career as a speaker and trainer, when I temporarily stopped hiding behind facts, figures, or information-heavy slide decks and gave myself permission to be in the liminal space between audience and stage. I even owe my marriage to the practice of Stop and Smile.

During the summer before my senior year of college, I let a

friend from an improv class convince me to go to a nightclub to watch him do stand-up. Although I've lived in Las Vegas for much of my life, I'm not much of a nightclub girl. I don't like long lines. I don't like crowds. And I don't like to be in environments where I feel like my drink is likely to be roofied.

But before this particular club officially opened on weekend nights, and throngs of drunk and sweaty local Las Vegas women squeezed into their tube tops and animal-print pleather hot pants to experience a night of debauchery with, in most cases, equally awkward young men, the club hosted open-mic nights for aspiring comedians. And during the aforementioned night, I breathed my way through half a dozen awkward sets, waiting for my friend to finally perform his, feeling seriously out of place in my baggy jeans and black tank top with sparkly red poinsettias. (I was a proud, card-carrying feminist, majoring in women's studies in the early aughts. I clearly didn't understand the concept of club wear.)

Anyway, when I thought I couldn't possibly feel any more uncomfortable, a man dressed as a filibuster, the official name for an antebellum pirate (which was this comic's character), made his way onto the stage to perform. The comic, who went by the stage name of Lafitte, invited a man up onto the stage to be a part of a bit. And for the next five minutes or so, Lafitte attempted to emasculate (at times it felt more like verbally flog) this man. You didn't need to be a Rhodes scholar to see that Lafitte was doing a poor job of masking some intense prejudices by taking on the identity of an angry pirate. He ridiculed this lone man of color in the audience — for his height, his job, and even for being part Hawaiian. And the man, well, he didn't take the bait and attack back. He didn't defend or even deflect. He stood under the spotlight, calmly and clearly answered the questions he was asked, smiled at the audience (all of whom were clearly on his side), smiled and connected with us more whenever he needed to find his words, and presented a quiet, unwavering confidence that compelled me to introduce myself to him afterward. And marry him six years later!

One of my favorite exercises to lead, typically at the end of a retreat or intensive experience, is called "When I Look at You, I See…" In this activity a participant stands before her group members, allowing herself to be both seen and acknowledged. For a couple of minutes, her peers popcorn around and share aloud what they see in this woman. Participants report that while they wish they didn't crave other people's validation, the act of standing and receiving other people's agenda-less opinions of them gives them permission to see themselves in their full power — often in a way they never have before.

Fortunately, you don't need to participate in this exercise live to experience the insights it typically awakens and the transformation it facilitates. (Although if you are inspired to lead the activity for other like-minded women, please do so.) In the meantime, you can give yourself your own opportunities to illuminate your many gifts and be fully present in your body when preparing to speak. I invite you to practice the following exercises and turn them into lifelong habits.

BUFF UP YOUR CAPACITY FOR VISIBILITY

1. Gratitude Mirror Work

Because you want other people to see and connect with you through your communication, it's vital that you learn how to see and truly connect with yourself first. If you've been jamming in the world of self-improvement for a while, it's likely you've learned about, and perhaps even experimented with, mirror work. It's also possible that if you started a mirror work practice, you didn't maintain it. As self-help pioneer Louise Hay confessed, "Mirror work can be very confronting at first. It reveals your most basic fear and your most terrible self-judgments. But if you keep looking in the mirror, you will begin to see through those judgments and see who you really are." In the following exercise, my goal is to get you through the discomfort as quickly as possible by giving your monkey mind a very specific objective — speaking self-gratitude.

Directions: Stand in front of a full-length mirror so that you can see your entire body. Take a moment to breathe, in through your nose and out through your mouth. Allow yourself to really see you — all of you. Then, when you are truly present, set a timer for sixty seconds. And during those sixty seconds, say aloud all that you are grateful to yourself for (my voice, my hands that take my message from my heart to my audience, my capacity for presence, my resilience). Go deep — and don't force a specific answer! Allow whatever comes up to be spoken. I recommend that you repeat this exercise daily for at least three weeks (increasing your time in the mirror day by day in thirty-second increments until you get to at least five minutes). Then, after the three weeks, maintain your practice by scheduling yourself for gratitude mirror work at least three times a week — and always before you have something important to communicate interpersonally or onstage.

2. Dance the Demons Out

While many of us with a dance background have been socialized to view dance as a competitive sport — in which our desire for perfection trumps our experience of presence and stymies our capacity for flow — dance can (and in my humble opinion *should*) be a catalyst for dynamic communication. Dance can be a vehicle to reawaken our bodies, turn down the volume on our unhelpful self-talk, and connect us with a power greater than ourselves so that we can play nicely with the sensations we experience around visibility. Whenever you want to drop down from your head into your body, particularly in the moments when you are sculpting a message you want to communicate powerfully, give yourself ten minutes to dance the demons out.

Directions: Find yourself a private space in your home or office, dim the lights (and light some candles), turn on some of your favorite tunes, and let your body move the way it's aching to. If you consider yourself a dancer, replace the need to choreograph with an invitation to cocreate with the divine. Whenever you feel sensation pooling in certain areas, or your brain wants to colonize the rest of your body, give yourself a dance break. Afterward, when you revisit your communication, note how an awakened body and endorphin rush positively impact what you devise and rehearse.

3. Self-Service Visualization

While physical movement supports mind-body-soul integration and can quickly shift our experience of sensation from anxiety to moxie, after moving our bodies it's vital to give ourselves some quiet time to hear (versus force) the messages and specific words we want to communicate. Guided visualization is one of my favorite strategies for this.

Directions: When we hear the word *selfish*, we usually think of the word's negative connotations. For we've been socialized to think of avoiding selfishness at all costs. As a result, we have internalized the message that when we honor ourselves, we do so at the expense of serving others. The opposite is actually true. We must serve our deepest needs and desires to be of maximum service in the world. To speak powerfully and to be heard accurately. Download and participate in my Self-Service Visualization at AlexiaVernon.com /MoxieBook to quiet your mind, open your heart, reconnect with the many ways you shine, and empower heart-centered, high-impact communication.

QUESTIONS FOR REFLECTION

- What are you grateful to yourself for?
- What do you know is true — about your voice, your gifts, and who you are called to be (and what you are called to say) in the world?
- How is visibility not only an opportunity but also a responsibility for you?
- As a result of turning the practices in this chapter into habits, how is your experience of your sensation evolving?
- How is your communication transforming?

Most of us get in the way of our own confident, competent, and conscious communication. We have spent so long trying to be who we think we are supposed to be that we have forgotten how to speak as our authentic selves and be truly seen by the people we are seeking to affect. We strive to be likable — but not too people-pleasing. Confident — but not vain. Funny — but not too much of a ham. As a result, most of us are in our heads, trying to memorize our words and our mannerisms, thereby becoming more connected to our self-talk than to our audiences.

The best communicators don't *perform*. We get in front of our audiences and are *present* — to everything we are feeling, to what's happening in the room (or onstage), and to the intuitive downloads we are receiving (and reacting to and from).

Cultivating communication presence is often as much about

what we *stop doing* as it is about what we focus on. After all, it's our drive for an unattainable level of perfection that often messes with our ability to be us. And to tell our truth. In the next chapter, I'll explain why it took me nearly thirty years to start telling my truth, and I'll invite you to start telling yours. As I've been known to say, "The world doesn't need more experts, but it does need more soul stirrers."

CHAPTER 9

WHAT TO SAY WHEN
THE SPOTLIGHT IS YOURS

We love seeing raw truth and openness in other people, but we're afraid to let them see it in us. We're afraid that our truth isn't enough — that what we have to offer isn't enough without the bells and whistles, without editing, and impressing.

— BRENÉ BROWN

When I read Shonda Rhimes's memoir, *Year of Yes*, I connected immediately to the idea of being, like the author, an unreliable narrator. Only, for the first quarter of my life, I wasn't seeking to entertain anyone with my half-truths. Rather, I had gotten so good at editing out painful episodes from my memory that I struggled to discern fact from fiction. Although, deep within my cells, of course, I had never truly forgotten, even if I had for the most part forgiven.

The first time I stepped into my moxie, I was four years old. It was Christmas, and every year while they were married, much to my mother's chagrin, my dad would host a big shindig at our house. Depending on the year, extended family, neighbors, friends, and even my dad's employees would come by for a holiday dinner. And this particular Christmas, after everyone had gone home and my parents were asleep in their bedroom, I lay in my new big-kid bed in my bedroom across the hall, unable to sleep. For I had made a promise that night to keep a secret. And even though this was back in the day before the expression "snitches get stitches," I still got the message loud and clear that if I spoke up, there would be serious consequences. And yet, even though I was a preschooler, my body had already begun to speak to me. And my body, specifically my tummy, was saying, *Lex, you've got to say something.*

I got myself out of bed, creeped across the hallway to my parents' bedroom, woke them up, and shared with them what I know, as the mom of a daughter who is now the exact same age that I was at the time, is the worst information a parent could hear from her child. I told them that somebody in our family was touching me *down there*, I didn't want to keep the secret anymore, and I wanted them to make it stop.

I wish I could tell you that that initial act of moxie created the foundation for a lifetime of speaking up and out, but as you know it most definitely did not. Not everyone in my family was ready for the difficult information that I delivered, and I watched a lot of people I loved struggle with my revelation. Those are *their* stories, however, and not mine. What matters was the message I took away, and the impact it had on me.

When you speak, people listen, Lex. And your words create impact.

And I wasn't sure I wanted that level of responsibility. So while my mom, as a nurse and as my fiercest advocate — then, and every day of my life before and after — ensured that I got into the best treatment program and started the healing process, I saw how broken she became in the aftermath of my disclosure. I saw how other family members felt forced to choose between me and the family member who had been molesting me. As I grew up, I very consciously chose to archive the files connected to what happened in a difficult, if not impossible-to-reach storage area — and tried with all my might to lose the key. I began the narrative of my journey to my own voice with my current-events speech. While not a feel-good speaking moment by any means, it felt like a much safer place to start.

After my high school retreat, where I first shared my abuse story publicly and started to play with my new, more comprehensive narrative, I attempted several years later to tell it again via a spoken-word event. The day of my performance I woke up with laryngitis, and somebody else told my story for me. It would take me almost another decade to share the story in a speech again. And even after I launched my coaching business, I had a pattern of hiding as a speaker. I hid behind what experts said rather than articulating my own fresh viewpoints. When I spoke, I relied too heavily on statistics, case studies, and research. And even when I told stories, I used humor as armor to hide my messy feelings. Nobody saw the real me. How could they? I didn't give myself permission to listen to what I was aching to say aloud. Because if I did, it would have meant going way back and pulling out those old files, dusting them off, and making meaning out of them — for myself first, and then for my audiences.

As a result, I allowed my speaking, my business, and ultimately my identity to be shaped by what others projected onto me — and who I thought others wanted me to be. I very successfully played the role of a career expert, millennial expert, and onboarding expert, seeking to fill openings rather than creating my own opportunities. I booked clients, speaking gigs, and media segments in which I circled around the perimeter of my purpose, always telling myself, *Once you hit X benchmark, Lex, then you can transition into more transformational work where you can be yourself.*

Have you given yourself parameters for where (or when) you can say, do, or be the real you?

It leaves you feeling like a messy wax figure of yourself, doesn't it?

Shortly after the pitch fest I described in the introduction, when I felt a light turn on inside me and knew that I was supposed to support women to step into their moxie, I got asked to give a TED-style talk at a local event. I was told I could pick any topic, as long as it related to my pathway to happiness. I chose forgiveness. I don't profess to be an expert on forgiveness and, much to my surprise, this delighted the event organizers. "We don't need you to be an expert, Lex. We want you to tell a story about why forgiveness has led you to happiness."

As the reality set in regarding what I had committed to, for there was no hiding in *that* story, the usual sensation and self-talk that cropped up each time I agreed to a speaking engagement, corporate training, or consulting project was notably missing. *I don't have to puff up, prove myself, and people-please. I get to surrender and speak my truth.*

On the night of the gig, I was informed that a hotshot entrepreneur and speaker, with an affinity for dropping f-bombs like Beyoncé drops number-one hits, was in town and that he would be speaking before me. Some guys sitting in the audience made a drinking game of sipping beer every time said speaker cussed, and I'm pretty sure they were reordering their pints halfway in. And yet the bigger, cruder, and more hustle-y the speaker became, the more I softened into my body, my message, and my certainty that what I had to say would be equally valued, even in a room that was three-fourths twentysomething tech dudes.

When it was my turn to speak, I felt the awesomeness of the opportunity before me as I walked to the makeshift stage at the front of the coffeehouse where the event took place. I paused at least half a minute before I began, taking in the crowd, making eye contact with an audience that had exploded from standing room only to people pushed out the door, listening from the street. I imagined this was what it felt like to be a rock star, only the celebrity everyone was there to see had opened for *me*. I let myself articulate my awe with a few too many "wows," and then launched into my story, sharing how I had forgiven my family members who had committed, or been complicit in, my sexual abuse. And how choosing to forgive, and more important, practicing forgiveness, in prayer, meditation, visualization — even when my heart couldn't forgive as fully as my brain could — ultimately enabled me to melt away the rage I had been holding on to. That for years was harming me far more, I suspected, than it was harming anyone else in my family.

I revealed, like a giddy schoolgirl, the benefits I was experiencing as I cultivated and put into action my daily forgiveness practice — how I felt lighter and more creative, joyful, mindful, spiritual, and in my voice. I revealed how every day I chose to sever negative thoughts and stories about others in my life, even if it took time for my feelings to follow suit, because I would no longer tolerate the misery that came from the conflation of holding people accountable and holding them (and myself) in judgment and contempt.

When I finished and came back to my seat, I was thrust back into a state of awe. Both women and men approached me, some sharing their own strikingly familiar abuse stories, others sharing with me their own speaking dreams. I held space for a lot of healing (and dreaming) that night. *This* was what I was built for. Sharing my story. Inviting other people to access and, in many cases, start the process of healing their own. Speaking just happened to be my medium. When I launched my first in-person group speaker coaching program a few months later, it filled quickly, and many of the participants in my live programs over the next few years were in the room that game-changing evening.

Tell Stories to Ignite Discovery in Your Audience

While I don't envision that I (or you) will live until an age when public speaking is not one of most people's greatest fears, it's thrilling to live in an age when so many people still have a dream to get onstage and speak. Most of the speakers I have supported over the years, and there have been thousands of them, do not say they want to speak, or improve their speaking ability, because they are so smart and talented and they feel the responsibility to share their volumes of wisdom with others. I share this not to suggest that my community members have low self-esteem or a lack of worthiness; although, a fair number of speakers I have worked with do struggle with their self-confidence, to be sure. Rather, I want to highlight what catalyzes their desire to speak: their desire to *serve*.

From dreaming of giving a TED Talk or keynote speech, to aspiring to speak at one's professional association or lead a breakout session at an industry conference, to wanting to speak on a community leadership panel or present in front of fellow employees, most women (and men) share that even though they're not quite sure how they will put their voices out into the world and onto stages in bigger ways, their reason for doing it is to inspire others and make a positive impact. And yet they retreat from one of the greatest tools they have at their disposal — stories.

If you want to speak, and in some way transform the lives of others, you *must* use stories that show your audiences how to cultivate the mindset, heartset, behaviors, skills, and habits to be successful in whatever area you want them to be successful. The kinds of Come to Jesus stories you identified in the first chapter work swimmingly for this. The stories you recalled, relived, reframed, released (and are, I hope, reapplying) are the kinds of stories you want to be sharing when you get in front of *most* audiences to speak. Now, if you are speaking at a staff meeting, your story may be less personal and more professional; but even still, stories have a place, and they can be used to influence and bring about transformation.

Our Come to Jesus stories are so powerful for an audience because these stories have brought us to our knees — and redefined us. They have shown us how to go from seeing ourselves and our place in the world in black-and-white to seeing in Technicolor, or even 3-D. And most important, these are often the very kinds of stories the people we are seeking to impact are stuck in, even if the specific details are different. When we share our stories, specifically how we have reframed, released, and reapplied what we have discovered, we invite our audience members to have their own realizations and potential aha moments.

Where many of my clients, and speakers in general, run amok, is in mistaking their stories for their big ideas, or using stories in a way that comes across as ego-based. "I cut off my own foot to survive gangrene, which I contracted while volunteering with refugee children, so anything you've ever gone through is peanuts compared to my trauma." Or it feels manipulative. "Let me tell you about how I went from welfare to millionaire in just over eighteen months. Great, now hire me to show you how to trade food stamps for foie gras." Or, best-case scenario, it feels like a story with no value to an audience beyond entertainment.

"Listen to my twenty-minute story about my family reunion. I have twelve crazy uncles…womp womp."

While I integrate numerous Come to Jesus stories into my presentations and trainings, I also drop in plenty of everyday stories — mined from running my business, parenting my daughter, cutting my toenails. You don't need to have lived through great tragedy or epic events to tell stories that illuminate important concepts and inspire listeners to take action. The key to any story, as we'll explore, is using your stories as an ingredient in moving your audience to action, not as the meal itself. As a former TEDx organizer, I encourage any speaker I work with to identify what TED calls their "idea worth spreading" — the big idea they are advancing. That is the focus of a presentation, and stories and any other source material you bring in (quotes, research, questions, case studies) are designed to support it.

Let's return to our company staff meeting example. If you are speaking in front of employees, your big idea may not feel like it's big outside your organization's four walls. But "It's time to start a company recycling program" or even something really mundane like "I'd like to change pencil providers because the erasers we have are crummy" is still the idea you want to spread, even if it won't lead you onto a TED stage. Whether you are waxing poetic about recycling or rubber, stories matter, even if they are more pedestrian than heart-wrenching.

For a lot of speakers who want to give business presentations or motivational speeches, it can be terrifying (and at times can feel mildly trauma inducing) to declare, "This big idea is mine, and mine alone." It's easy to get paralyzed or to engage our Critic and ask, "Will anyone care? How can I distill everything I'm passionate about into one idea? Hasn't somebody/everybody already said this before?" To soothe the monkey mind, and all the crap that such a mind produces, I recommend that when creating a

presentation, you sit with a few questions before starting to orga-
nize your ideas. Here are some of my favorites:

- What topics am I passionate about, and what theme runs
  through most of them?
- What topics are big in my industry, and what viewpoint
  do I have on one or more of those topics that disrupts the
  status quo?
- What's something that really bugs me about my industry?
- What's the most important thing for someone to take
  away from the presentation I want to give?
- What stories does my audience need to hear from me to
  ensure they have this takeaway?

Once you sit with your answers to these questions and start to
see the big idea you want to communicate, then state it succinctly:

The idea that I want my audience to take action on is

_____.

(If you can't condense your big idea into one sentence, that's
a good indication you haven't refined the idea enough to develop
it into a presentation.)

Then I recommend working backward, as we explored in
chapter 6. What needs to come before your call to action? What
would you say before that? And before that? Continue to work
backward until you rewind yourself to the beginning and establish
your opening. Now, it's highly unlikely you will come up with a
nuanced, effective, fully realized presentation from your first pass
at an outline. Creative work — be it writing, speaking, or blowing
glass — takes the time it takes. However, this process of beginning
with the end in mind and reverse-engineering, and curating stories,
experiences, and evidence, will ensure that when the spotlight is
yours, you will be clear about what you are communicating.

Let's come back to story. After you have reverse-engineered, you likely have come up with places where you have identified that a story would be effective. The way you sculpt a story, choose the details you will share, and ultimately bring your audience into your story will play a central role in how your audience connects with you and, as a result, the likelihood of their following your call to action. While entire books have been written on how to tell a story, I like to keep storytelling for the stage (or a speech) as simple as possible. Before I decide to use a story in a speech, workshop, or class, or in any other teaching format, I identify:

What's the aha moment I would love for my audience to have?

I didn't wake up one day and decide I should start telling the story I shared in chapter 1, for example, about the debacle of my first speech. I selected the story, and have continued to tell it for many years, because I first decided I wanted each of my audience members to realize the impact of the story *she* has created about who she is as a communicator. As you'll see in the following description, I selected the story because it best showed that idea. Then, because you know I love to reverse-engineer, after honing in on my desired discovery for my audience, I asked myself:

What's a question (or series of questions) I can ask that would likely prompt the realization I'm seeking?

You may recall that I asked you a few interrelated questions as I wound down my current-events story. *What story have you been carrying around about who you are as a communicator? Is that story setting you up to show up, speak up, and be seen in the world?* We'll come back to how you will use *your* question (or series of questions) shortly. Afterward, I consider:

What story shows me or a client, person in the news, or figure from history going through a process that led to the kind of aha moment I'm hoping for my audience to have? Or shows a person (usually me) making the mistakes / experiencing the difficulties that are likely occurring for my audience?

These last two interrelated questions are important, because without the answers, though you might be telling a great story, the story is unlikely to facilitate transformation for your audience. It was going through this process that sparked the realization that the current-events story needed to be a part of my presentations.

Finally, you consider:

What details do I select and incorporate when I tell my story so that it can create insight and transformation for my audience? And how do I transition from me, and my story, back to my audience?

You actually have the answer to the second part of this question, even if it needs a bit of refinement. The way you give your story over to your audience is by inviting each person listening to move into the role of protagonist. How do you do that? By asking your audience the question or series of questions you've just identified. It's in those questions that the deepest insights for your audience happen.

USE A STORY TO FACILITATE AN AHA

Now it's time to go through the process outlined above to identify a story you could use as a focal point in a presentation to ignite discovery in your audience. (And then, whether your audience consists of your coworkers, members of your professional association, or attendees at a conference or community event, go out and deliver it for them!)

Directions: Answer the following questions to identify the transformation you want to create for your audience, and then choose the best story to help you do it.

- What's the aha moment I would love for my audience to have?
- What question (or series of questions) can I ask that would prompt the realization I'm seeking?
- What story shows me, a client, a person in the news, or a figure from history going through a process that led to the kind of aha moment I'm hoping for my audience to have?
- What details from my story do I need to tell to create insight and transformation for my audience?

QUESTIONS FOR REFLECTION

- How does it feel to use stories to create discovery for an audience?
- How do people react to the stories you tell and the questions you ask?
- As you incorporate stories into your communication, what do you observe about your ability to connect with and move people to take action?

When clients ask me, "Does the sensation of being seen by an audience ever get easier?" I'm glad I can stand in my integrity and say, "Yes." Learning how to be present with the sensation that comes up when being seen (and thinking of being seen) by an audience played a pivotal role in the development of my moxie as a speaker. As did learning how to tell stories that allowed me to drop the expert shtick and focus on connecting with an audience (and laying the tracks for their transformation). Any time I feel wiggly inside, I make sure I am telling stories and asking questions that ignite discovery for my audience — and that I'm doing enough role-playing of those stories and questions before I have a true audience to speak to. The sooner I stop trying to impress, or worse, evaluate my performance, and instead start focusing on my audience and where I want *them* to go, the better I feel and the more compelling I am with my communication — in conversations and presentations.

There is one communication context, however, in which I still sometimes struggle to play nicely with the sensation that comes up. While I no longer hold my breath in situations when I sense that conflict is looming, it's still the area of communication where I have the most room for evolution. While I haven't succeeded in quelling all the grossness that emerges when real or perceived conflict does transpire, fortunately I've identified and developed the habits that allow me to make the necessary conversations at these times more daring than difficult. In the next chapter, I'll show you how to break up with any fear you may have about speaking up when conflict rears its ugly head.

CONFLICT IS THE PITS, UNTIL IT ISN'T

Conflict cannot survive without your participation.

— WAYNE DYER

When I was growing up, Thanksgiving was an *interesting* holiday in my family. One year my mom threw a turkey in the direction of my dad — after he had asked her a few too many times when it would be ready. (I have a feeling most women have wanted to do something like this, but only my mom had the moxie to actually do it!) Another year I had a massive nasal hemorrhage and wound up in the emergency room to get a life-saving noseclip. But the Thanksgiving that definitely tops all others for being memorable was the year my parents decided to divorce. Most kids do not want their parents to split up. I was not one of those kids. Even though in first grade, after a friend's parents divorced and she was devastated, I begged my parents to swear they'd be together forever, not too long afterward I got a sense that life might be easier on all of us if my parents took back their promise.

Now, I know I'm lucky. My parents were never bashful regarding their adoration of me. And I love both my parents very much. I'm glad that in later years they have become friends again, swapping orthopedic shoe and neurologist recommendations. But jeepers, during the first decade of my life, my parents were bad news if there weren't several states between them. So when I was eight years old, and I came out of my bedroom on Thanksgiving morning to see my parents sitting in our newly remodeled kitchen next to each other, reading the paper and sipping coffee, something felt off. For the Cleavers Mr. and Mrs. Vernon were not. One of them mentioned, casually, like the way you'd say, "I'm going to go check the mail" or "Can you pass the salt and pepper?" that they were getting divorced. Even though their behavior on our most recent family vacation indicated that something like this could be coming, I was surprised. Not so much by the revelation but rather by the breeziness of the announcement.

Fast-forward to Thanksgiving dinner that evening. My parents, who earlier professed to be aligned in their decision not to adjust our holiday plans, grew increasingly cold with each other on our drive over to the house of some friends of my aunt's and uncle's. Each person seated at the excruciatingly long dinner table expressed gratitude. These were primarily Hollywood folks, so there was a lot of, "Thank you very much, God, for seeing that my latest picture got backed." "Thanks for the Emmy. No matter how many you receive, it's still an honor." And then it got around to my motley crew.

My dad said something super snarky, and since this is my book and not his, I'm going to leave that detail out. My mom, justifiably stunned and humiliated, kicked him under the table. Hard. And within the next ninety seconds, wine was thrown, my dad was chased out of the house (by my mom; I probably didn't need to tell you that). And as my aunt followed them out the door to chaperone their paparazzi-worthy fight, I remember sitting at the table next to my uncle, and three dozen of his closest friends thinking, *My parents are batshit crazy.* Or the eight-year-old version of that.

For years if I so much as smelled the possibility of conflict brewing, I used my earthquake preparedness training and would "stop, drop, and hold." Internally. This translated into not speaking up for myself when my boundaries were trampled on, swallowing my desires, and losing heaps of professional and personal relationships because I let awkward situations go unaddressed until the people in them disappeared from my life. It also created years of stomach pains and tension headaches, and it fueled much of my icky self-talk.

For most of us, the conflict we primarily encounter is not the kind of conflict I witnessed at that fateful Thanksgiving dinner. Thankfully, those moments are rare. And when they happen, usually there is little we can do other than breathe through the intensity of the moment, reach out to our loved ones for support, and then, once emotions have settled down, heal ourselves, and if possible, strive to heal the relationships involved. However, it's the conflict that is happening in our inner world (when we construct the worst possible scenario for a conversation, relationship, or situation and replay it over and over again like a 1990s mixtape) that we should be the most concerned about.

The Conflict We Create

It might sound harsh of me to suggest that you are responsible for much of the conflict you experience, but hopefully there's also something liberating in it. If you're creating your hell, you can alternatively create your heaven. (That sounded way less cheesy in my head.) What I do mean is that when you find yourself in situations in which you know conflict is possible, and similarly know that a conversation needs to happen to prevent you from feeling like you are trying to tread water in a sinkhole, you have four choices.

1. You can avoid the conversation. I bet you can guess what I think about this option. In case you can't, it's on par with what I think about eating deep-fried tarantulas. Yes, that's actually a thing. You can look it up if you don't believe me.

2. You can wing the conversation. Because winging things usually works. Doctors wing surgeries. Lawyers wing litigation. And actors wing their lines. Okay, actors sometimes do that, but you get my point.

3. You can mentally script what you plan to say, and have the conversation over and over in your head. Please don't try this option unless you enjoy eating foods you have an anaphylactic reaction to.

4. You can plan out your conversation, role-play it, and then show up and have it. Winner winner, chicken dinner!

Clearly, number 4 is the best option. But because you are most likely not choosing it, you often default to feeling like you are growing the next world war in a petri dish — and that petri dish just so happens to live in your body. However, it's not enough for me to say, "Choose option 4." I get it. To help make it feel like a viable option, I need to give you something (actually a few things), so let me start with a critical reframe. I want you to shift from seeing the kind of conversation you know you need to have as "difficult" to seeing it as "daring." For *difficult* conversations happen when you see yourself as the recipient of conflict (real or perceived) rather than as the cocreator of your situation. When you choose compassion, curiosity, creativity, and collaboration, you shift a difficult conversation into a daring one.

Having led programs on interpersonal communication and public speaking for years, I have geeked out on my fair share of "how to navigate through conflict" courses and books. Truthfully, while many of the recommendations are good and can work, many don't have a chance of working because they involve to-dos that are far too complicated for us to pull off when we are gestating an anxiety baby in our body because a coworker or client is acting like a dodo-head. Our way out of paralysis, in the moments when we feel like we are on a road to nowhere (or when we see something and know we have to say something, as Homeland Security would advise), is to have a few guideposts that allow us to sculpt, speak, and then surrender.

How to Prepare for a Daring Conversation

The key to having a daring conversation is giving yourself enough time to properly prepare for one — but not so much time that you never have it, or that by the time you have it, the person you are speaking with either has no idea what you are talking about or the situation that was such a big deal to us didn't even register on her Richter scale. While time is subjective, and the ten to twenty minutes of sensation I feel before I speak may feel like twenty eternities in purgatory for someone who is brand-new to speaking, when it comes to a daring conversation, as a rule it's best to have it within a week of deciding your organs could finally unstick themselves if you said something. And before you do, here is how you can set up yourself, and the other parties involved, for success.

First, schedule the conversation. If you're not going to wing it, nobody else involved should, either. Give the person or people you are going to speak with a heads-up that you'd like to speak. And then prepare:

Reverse-engineer what you want to say from your desired outcome. You should be masterful at doing this by now!

Identify the questions you can ask to learn other people's truth. It's easy to go into a daring conversation with a laundry list of complaints. Or assumptions. Instead, for each thing that triggers you, pull out of the emotion and find a question or two so you can investigate what is going on for the other party.

Distinguish what you are entitled to say from what you want to say. As a kiddo, I had several stints in therapy. It was one of the few spaces where I could unload all my pent-up emotions. Bang things. Occasionally break things. And more important, say the things I was too petrified to say to the people I wanted to be saying them to. One of my therapists told me, and I was too young at the time to appreciate it, that while I could scream profanities at a certain family member, if we ever did have a daring conversation that probably wouldn't move me toward what I really wanted — for the person to acknowledge and take responsibility for his actions. Now that it's decades later, I *always* give myself time and space to speak my vitriol, especially when somebody has truly wronged me. I just strive to do it without an audience, because it never serves me to attack another person, especially someone I want something from — irrespective of how entitled I feel I am to do so. And if and when a daring conversation doesn't go the way I intend, and someone lashes out at me, I (usually) resist the temptation to attack back. Instead, I assert myself and then stand in my power via silence.

Speak your words. If you're anything like who I used to be, you spend a lot of time thinking about what you want to say, but you don't always default to practicing your words out loud. When you verbalize what you plan to say, you minimize ruminating. And you ensure that when you do speak, you actually say what you intended to say — so that your words have the maximum possible positive impact.

Bless and release — before you say anything. It's difficult, if not impossible, to have a true daring conversation with someone when you are still enmeshed in anger toward them. When you see yourself as a victim or martyr and someone else as somebody who "did something to you." One of my favorite Oprah-isms is "Forgiveness is giving up the hope that the past could have been any different. It's accepting the past for what it was, and using this moment and this time to help yourself move forward." You don't need to let anybody off the hook for his or her actions, but you need to be fully in the role of protagonist and ready to move forward if you are going to have a productive conversation with the person.

Play nicely with the sensation that thoughts of your daring conversation elicit. Please revisit chapter 8 if you need a reminder of the many tools available to you. Daring conversations can be emotionally and physiologically triggering. Nonetheless, they are an important way to step into our moxie.

How to Cocreate a Daring Conversation

When you do have your daring conversations, show up knowing that the only thing you can control is — how you show up. What you say. Whether you react (by immediately acting from your feelings) or respond (by observing how you are feeling and then intentionally deciding what you want to do about it). Really, this is something to remember in all communication moments. For the sad truth is, someone in our professional or personal lives can unfortunately lash out at us when we least expect it — or when we do expect it but are nonetheless not verbally prepared for it.

Having had enough daring conversations in my life to have a PhD in them, what I know is that the best ones are *always* when I walk away proud of my behavior — regardless of how the conversations ended. And, of course, the more I show up, speak, and behave from a place of compassionate vulnerability, the better the conversations usually (but not always) go.

Use direct communication to establish your agenda and the ways you are committed to behaving. It's easy to assume that because the blood coursing through your veins has volcanic potential, surely everybody you're speaking with knows what you're there to talk about. That's not always the case. State your reasons for wanting to chat, and your priorities, and set a daring-conversation tone by sharing the kind of communication you are committed to putting forward. When you model daring behavior, you set up everyone else to go daring too.

Ask other parties for their input. Daring conversations are cocreated. While you might be taking the lead (because you are someone who unapologetically steps into her moxie), after you share what you want, be sure to give space for others to share as well.

Share your story, and ask about others' points of view. You set up the conversation, so despite how uncomfortable it may feel, you need to tell your version of events (or your point of view on a current situation) to move the conversation forward. Once you survive the initial discomfort of speaking up, you are curious (yes, I possess some bias here; I want you to be curious), and therefore, it's time to ask how the other person (or people) sees what has happened.

Choose tone and nonverbal body language that demonstrate your commitment to maintaining respect and promoting genuine understanding. You want to use facial expressions, gestures, and posture (particularly when you are listening and receiving information that triggers emotion from you) that keep the conversation daring. If you feel your mouth and jaw contorting into RBF (yes, that's resting bitch face), use your breath to relax. If you feel your shoulders collapsing in, or climbing an imaginary ladder up to your ears, use your breath to relax. If your legs are wrapped around each other like peanut butter searching for its jelly, yup, use your breath to relax.

As you move into sharing your respective truths, identify misunderstandings and what you have learned. As your conversation progresses, and you realize that what you so clearly thought was spaghetti was asparagus soup for the other party, take responsibility for your role in what has happened. And more important, declare how you are committed to moving forward. (This does *not* mean going bunny and apologizing for something you believe, or know!, you did not do. This means going cheetah and owning legitimate mistakes when you make them — or your part in situations where you see you could have done better.)

Discuss creative ways for playing nicely together in the future. A daring conversation, in my book, which this is, gets the stamp of success when all parties are able to get along with each other during the conversation, cocreate the space to speak what needs to be shared and moved through, and walk away clear on their roles in maintaining the peace in the future. I strive never to end a daring conversation until I've said everything I prepared to communicate, and I've asked, and everyone involved has answered, "How do we ensure we never need to have this particular conversation again?"

Words and Phrases That Keep Conversations Daring

The words that we use, from moment to moment, in a conversation where conflict could transpire (or has transpired) often determine whether things go difficult or daring. I recommend using the following words as often as possible:

Yes. My favorite agreement word. Ever. It makes someone instantly feel seen and heard. You can say "yes" after someone shares an idea, an opinion, or a feeling, but do refrain from saying "yes and" and then redirecting the conversation back to you. "Yes and" works great in comedy, but "yes" as a complete sentence usually works better in daring conversations.

Thank you. You can say "thank you" to someone for sharing where she is coming from, for being vulnerable, for telling you the truth, for helping you understand her perspective, or for acknowledging wrongdoing or committing to better behavior in the future.

What I want for *us* is... These words work great for communicating what you want from the conversation. Try not to use them to linguistically wrestle for power over someone but rather to propose something that the other person, no matter his or her perspective, likely wants too.

Tell me more. This phrase works whenever people are dropping into vulnerability and you want them to know you really want to hear what's going on, even if it's uncomfortable. Or, on the flip side, this short phrase is effective when you want to nudge people beyond surface talk so they can go to the source of what's truly going on.

I'm sorry. This is a very appropriate response when you have truly done something wrong, you want to take responsibility for it, and even more important, you want to communicate what you will do differently moving forward. Sometimes you may be sorry for the way someone is feeling, or the way you unintentionally made her or him feel — even if you haven't done anything super sorry-worthy. Be clear on what you are sorry for, and state *that*. (Again, please don't think I'm giving you a hall pass for giving your power away. The kind of "I'm sorry" I'm recommending here is different from the "I'm sorry" you use when you feel insecure or actually want someone else to apologize to you. "I'm sorry" must not be a quid pro quo.)

What do you need (from me) in order to move forward? When you brainstorm creative ways to play nicely together in the future, the ultimate expression of compassionate (and super vulnerable) power is to ask what someone else would like to see from you now and in the future. This question alone can resurrect a relationship from collapse, if and when safety has been created in a conversation and everyone is fully committed to a mutually beneficial outcome.

Words and Phrases That Keep Conversations Difficult

On the flip side, I recommend avoiding, at all costs, the following words and phrases, regardless of how entitled you feel to use them or how hooked into them you have been in the past. Why? Because they build a wall between you and the other party — and they are a direct flight back from the land of daring to the land of difficult:

A lot of _yous_ (especially when the conversation is past-oriented). The word _you_ often lands as an accusation and can trigger defensive and blaming behavior. Instead, strive to use the word _we_. Collective language, whether it's about what's happened in the past or what you are committing to in the future, keeps conversations daring.

That's not what I... It's easy to go all antagonized attack dog when someone misuses or misinterprets what you have said. Should this happen, calmly (and silently) note the misunderstanding to yourself. Somebody is not receiving the message you are intending to send. Instead of pulling out the claws and taking a bite, take a breath, and then use appropriate words and phrases from the preceding section to explain yourself again. The more uncomplicated you make your second attempt, the more likely it is that your message will be interpreted correctly.

That's not *my* problem/responsibility (or that's *your* problem/responsibility). Though this is an ugly cousin of the last phrase, I'm calling this one out separately. Because no matter whose problem or responsibility something is (or isn't), stating this (even if you are entitled to), is like lighting a match by a gas line outside your house and wondering why you burned your entire neighborhood down.

[Something conciliatory] but... No more *buts* in high-stakes conversations! As we explored in chapter 4, a *but* negates everything that has come before it. And when you have one foot in a difficult conversation and the other in a daring one, this word can pull you back into the former faster than a preschooler can get her entire family sick during cold and flu season. (I *may* be wearing a face mask as I write this chapter. Trust the analogy. It's as tight as my mask.)

[So-and-so] said... Please avoid gossip and triangulation. Leave third and fourth parties out. All that matters is what's transpiring right now, between you and the other person or parties before you. If you need to address somebody else's role in a situation, set up a separate time and a separate daring conversation for that.

When You're Triggered, Go to the Root

Addressing conflict head-on (and, more important, heart-on) can save women from medaling in self-reproach. Understanding why we are experiencing what we are from others plays an equally profound role in changing our relationship to conflict, separating our worthiness from how other people are behaving, and stretching our capacity for moment-to-moment (and long-term) forgiveness. Most people's behavior is not what it appears to be, even if what we see is ugly, painful, or at the very least, confusing.

This is a lesson I've had to learn every time (and there have been a lot of times) I wonder what the frick is going on with one of the trees in my yard. Living in the desert, I usually assume that when a tree stops thriving it's a dry-heat, underwatering problem. And then when a landscaping company comes out, I learn that the tree wasn't planted deeply enough, borers are feeding on bark, or there's a leak in the irrigation system and the tree is actually being chronically overwatered. In other words, I needed to look to the root for the answer, not the surface — or, to continue working the tree metaphor, at the branches and leaves.

Here's how you apply the same principle to the people in your life.

Manifestations of "Difficult" Behavior

Hiding Out

When people are hiding out, they may be avoiding conversations, meetings, or deadlines. And while if you look at the surface, it's easy to want to scream through a bullhorn, "Please stop slacking!" the reality is that this behavior is probably not the result of the person or people in question binge-watching their favorite TV series at night and having nothing left to give during the day.

LIKELY ROOT CAUSES
1. Not feeling competent.
2. Feeling unsafe.
3. Feeling unseen.

Solutions (Based on Root Causes)

1. Let people know where you see them performing well.
2. Create an environment where it's safe for people to speak up, take risks, and make mistakes.
3. Take the time to acknowledge and get to know people so they feel you are invested in their presence — because you are, right?

Checking Out

While this may look the same as hiding out — people seem disinterested, are chronically late, or flat-out miss things they are responsible for — when people act checked out, what they are actually communicating, when you dare (and have the patience) to go to the root, is: "Put me in, coach. Don't waste my potential!"

Likely Root Causes

1. Not feeling challenged.
2. Not feeling engaged.
3. People feel like you are all talk and no action.

Solutions (Based on Root Causes)

1. Stretch people just outside their comfort zone, so they can access their genius zone.
2. Discover people's motivators, and then play to them.
3. This one hurts, I know, but if people feel like you don't really care about their ideas, because they don't see their input leading to any action, it's time to let them know what is happening with their ideas. Even if they don't like the answer, it's better to know than not to.

Yelling

The audacity, for me to suggest that people who are yelling at you (or others) aren't just awful people. Well, they aren't. There's a reason for the hostility. As the daughter of a yeller (with yelling tendencies that I have to sleep eight hours a day to suppress), I can tell you why most people yell.

Likely Root Causes

1. Not feeling heard.
2. Not feeling powerful.
3. Modeling behaviors they've seen work for other people.

Solutions (Based on Root Causes)

1. Give people time to speak uninterrupted (but call out and cut off bullying behavior if it resurfaces).
2. Ask people where they are feeling out of control and what they need to feel in control (at least of their thoughts, choices, and behavior) again.
3. Explain the impact the behavior is having on you and/or others, and together cocreate a more mutually agreeable way to navigate unpleasant emotions. And, most important, ensure that you are addressing anyone else who yells in order to create an environment of consistency.

Blaming

Despite my growing fear that if I share that blaming is another behavior I'm striving to keep in remission, you will hesitate to keep reading my recommendations, I'm just going to say it. Okay, I guess I already did. This is another behavior I do when I'm triggered for one or more of the reasons I list below. So I know these root causes well, and I'm working on the solutions, with everything in me.

LIKELY ROOT CAUSES

1. Equating taking responsibility for wrongdoing with giving up power and prestige.
2. Feeling like a scapegoat.
3. Feeling frustrated by the status quo, other people's behaviors, and so on.

SOLUTIONS (BASED ON ROOT CAUSES)

1. Commend personal responsibility, even if it's for owning yucky thoughts, feelings, and behaviors.
2. Address everyone who played a role in a situation.
3. Grant permission and hold space for people to vent — and then help them move on.

Defending

"It wasn't me, I pinky-swear. Okay, I guess it could have been me, but I really don't think it was. Yeah, okay, so it was totally me." We defend for a variety of reasons. And to effectively cut off the behavior, we need to understand what the behavior stems from.

LIKELY ROOT CAUSES

1. Feeling attacked.
2. Feeling scared to tell the truth.
3. Projecting wrongdoing onto others.

SOLUTIONS (BASED ON ROOT CAUSES)

1. Avoid all the words and phrases that shift daring conversations back into difficult ones, especially the word *you*.
2. Make it safe for people to be transparent.

3. Model and, if appropriate, reward taking personal responsibility.

LOVE UP ON YOUR DIFFICULT PEOPLE

As you read about the five difficult behaviors, I bet the faces of people triggering you started to flash by faster than cards shuffled on a blackjack table. (I'm a Vegas girl; I needed to get in at least one gambling reference.) Yet, among all the faces, there was probably one that popped out more prominently than the rest. Stay with him or her for a moment.

Directions: Pick your number-one persona non grata, and name which difficult behavior(s) you are seeing. (It could be more than one!) Then pick the reason (or root cause) for each behavior, and pair it with the corresponding solution.

QUESTIONS FOR REFLECTION

*   How has this exercise shifted your perception of the person you identified?
*   When you apply your solution(s), how does the person's behavior evolve?
*   When you notice one of the five difficult behaviors in anyone, how will you respond (versus react) in the future?
*   What difficult behaviors do *you* default to?
*   What are your triggers, and how can you better respond when your buttons are pushed?

In this chapter I provided recommendations for what to do in everyday, little-*c* conflicts. Unfortunately, there may be times when external conflict is much bigger than the conflict you are creating in your head — or the conflict that erupts when you or someone you work, live, or serve alongside has a hiccup or two in judgment, 100 percent capital-*C* Conflict. According to the Childhood Domestic Violence Association, as of the time of this book's printing, five million children will witness domestic violence in a year in the United States, and forty million adult Americans grew up living with domestic violence. According to the US Department of Veterans Affairs, six out of every ten men (60 percent) and five out of every ten women (50 percent) experience trauma at some point in their lives. Not so surprisingly, then, approximately eight million adults have PTSD in any given year.

If you have experienced first- or secondhand physical, sexual, racial, verbal, or emotional violence — or witnessed someone's, particularly an authority figure's, gross misuse of power — a directive like, "Own your role, bless and release, and forgive" is tone-deaf at best, further traumatizing at worst. I am *not* suggesting that you strive to have a daring conversation with a perpetrator or take responsibility for your role in such a situation. What I want for you in these moments, when there is not, and cannot be, safety for such a conversation to happen, is to seek professional medical, therapeutic, and if appropriate, legal help. This is not a stepping-into-your-moxie issue. I've included recommended resources for you at AlexiaVernon.com/MoxieBook.

As we move into the final chapters of the book, we'll explore how to go from putting your voice out into the world (be it in presentations, in meetings, or in daring conversations in your work, home, or community) to using your influence to lead — in all corners of your life. We'll look at how to articulate your personal and professional boundaries and stay in your moxie in the moments that sneak up on you and threaten to suffocate you — when you think you've got it all together, you're rocking and rolling, and then all of a sudden, a pillowcase is thrown over your head, blinding you to everything you think you know about yourself while simultaneously robbing you of your oxygen supply. We'll look at how to stay in our moxie in these moments, and once we are on the other side, how to allow such moments to beckon us into an even greater expression of our leadership.

11

SUSAN B. ANTHONY DIDN'T FIGHT FOR YOUR RIGHT TO BE A MEANIE

I declare to you that woman must not depend upon the protection of man, but must be taught to protect herself, and there I take my stand.

— SUSAN B. ANTHONY

An abolitionist, educational reformer, labor activist, temperance worker, and suffragist, Susan B. Anthony (1820–1906) got more done in her eighty-six years of life, at a time when the average life expectancy in the United States was around fifty, than most of us could achieve if given two consecutive lifetimes to make our impact. A teacher by the age of seventeen, Anthony never married (which might have something to do with the scale of her activism and professional output — just sayin') and, among her many achievements, she partnered with Elizabeth Cady Stanton to lead the National American Woman Suffrage Association. In 1872 Anthony voted in her hometown of Rochester,

New York (which, as a reminder, was illegal at the time). She was arrested and convicted and worked with her pal Stanton to present Congress with a constitutional amendment giving women the right to vote. While Anthony would not live to see women in the United States earn the right to vote, what was known at the time as the Anthony Amendment would be signed into law as the Nineteenth Amendment to the US Constitution in 1920.

During my senior year of high school I learned who Susan B. Anthony was and about her prominent role in shaping the first wave of the American feminist movement. In history class that year, my classmates and I drew from a hat the name of a significant woman from US history. We were then tasked with performing a first-person monologue about her life. Some of the options included women like Anthony, Sojourner Truth, Betty Friedan, Gloria Steinem. Yours truly drew…Tracy Chapman.

I'm ashamed to admit this, but at the time I was devastated. I didn't know who Tracy Chapman was, and even when I learned that she is a folk singer–songwriter and social activist, I was still disappointed, and not just because I was terrified of the racial implications of telling the story of a woman of color. You see, I had just learned what feminism was, and I wanted more of a card-carrying feminist. Somebody like Anthony, who got arrested while advocating for women's rights. Or someone more contemporary who used words like *patriarchy* and *misogyny*, unapologetically. I wanted someone who could help me make sense of my sexual abuse, help me see that my experience was, unfortunately, very common for women — and men. From the moment that I heard feminism defined in my history class as the belief that there should be political, economic, and social equality, regardless of sex and gender, I was in. And I wanted to step into the shoes, and embody the voice, of someone who was as down with the f-word as I was.

During my second semester as an undergrad, I stumbled into a women's studies class, and shortly after, I changed my major. Then I joined the National Organization for Women (and even became a chapter leader for my city). Going to college in Las Vegas meant I was introduced to a feminism where I not only got to look at institutionalized and unconscious gender bias, or the at times messy intersections of sex and gender with race, class, sexual orientation, and ability; but I also got to study the liminal (a.k.a. blurry) space between sexual pleasure and danger — and I spent much of my college education debating whether sex work could be empowering. Still wrestling with my answer to that. I also chopped off my long hair, paraded my hairy underarms around on 100-plus-degree summer days, and told the guys I dated (now, to be fair, there were only three of them), that I was not down with the institution of marriage.

In addition to performing my feminism, I also did some more socially significant things, such as start a nonprofit leadership program for girls, become a campus sexual assault peer educator, and join the Gay-Straight Student Alliance and protest Minister Fred Phelps Sr. when he came to town espousing hate against the LGBTQ community. In graduate school, I crafted an interdisciplinary master of arts program that focused heavily on women's studies. And before I defended my graduate thesis, I lined up my first women's studies adjunct professor position.

Then, less than a year into my first full-time job, something happened. I started to get really angry. (Now, to be fair, in college my passion for addressing injustices was often construed as anger, but I always felt like I was effecting positive social change.) The anger I now felt, in my transition from grad school to full-time employment, was the anger of submission. Even though I worked for a nonprofit that was probably 90 percent female, and I worked alongside many feminists, I felt, let me come out and say it, oppressed. I definitely wouldn't use that word today. As a white, heterosexual, middle-class, able-bodied, supremely well-educated woman living in America, I want to slap my whiny, white-privileged, twentysomething millennial self for being more obtuse than any triangle could ever be, but that's how I felt at the time. As you know, at this point in my career I was supremely underearning — which is never fun, but particularly scary when you are strapped with massive student loan debt. I was a young professional, and much of my administrative work felt on par with the kind of domestic work that led many a second-wave feminist in the 1960s out of her home and onto the streets to march.

I had expected the workplace to be ground zero for growing my self-confidence. In college and grad school, I'd created a habit of overdelivering on people's expectations, creating my own leadership opportunities, and collecting accolades like a Venus fly-trap collects insects and arachnids. Yet, here I was with a graduate degree, spending more time making photocopies and schlepping to Dunkin' Donuts for coffee (albeit for female leaders) than I was capitalizing on all my lauded potential. I never felt like there was a right time to put my voice into an important conversation or raise my hand and challenge ideas or practices I found outdated or ineffective. And when a few years in I found my way out by becoming a coach, while I never stopped calling myself a feminist, I definitely questioned my identity as one — and equally questioned why the workplace, which was supposed to be my pathway toward liberation, had been a place where I felt repeatedly diminished.

Are You Part of the Angry Set?

A 2016 national survey by the *Washington Post* and the Kaiser Family Foundation found that six in ten women and approximately one-third of men call themselves feminists. For young women, the number is even higher. Sixty-four percent of young women between the ages of eighteen and thirty-four self-identify as feminists. However, 43 percent of Americans also see the feminist movement as angry. And I get that. I was an angry feminist. (To be clear, I'm still a feminist but not so angry anymore. Except when my kiddo parrots back something she's heard me say, like, "Mommy, I want you to take responsibility for your role in this situation" or my husband has a cold, and he acts like a sore throat and a runny nose is the man flu.)

Given that many of the women who are feminists, or at the very least subscribe to feminism's goals, are captured in the 43 percent stat, I think it's safe to say that too many women are struggling, profoundly, in their professional and personal lives — and they're (we're!) over it. And the feminism I have studied and taught can explain why women are peeved, at times self-hating, due to gender bias and a precarious process of socialization that begins the moment we are determined to be female. Yet feminism has, for the large part, failed to provide a pathway forward for individual women to simultaneously use our personal power and reclaim our happiness.

I don't care if you call yourself a feminist. Err…that's not entirely true. It would be dope if you were with the six in ten chickadees in Camp Feminist. What I want, even more, is for you to think about whether you are also part of the angry set. In other words, when you review your communication (including your self-talk) over the past month, can you recall saying (or doing) any of the following?

To Others

- "I'd love to _____, but I just don't have time."
- "Sure, I'll _____." (And afterward you cross off something you planned to do for yourself from your to-do list.)

- "I'm waiting to hear back from a few people before I know what my schedule looks like, so could you circle back around to me later?"
- Something impulsive and snarky you regretted as it came out of your mouth.
- Posting a straight-up nasty comment (not to be confused with constructive criticism) on social media about something or someone you didn't agree with.

To Yourself

- "Once I do _____, I'll be able to enjoy some downtime."
- "I wish that Al Gore, or whoever it really was, never invented the internet so I wouldn't have to reply to a bloody email ever again."
- "Does [insert a partner's or child's name] think I have nothing better to do than to clean up after him?"
- "Maybe if I 'accidentally' fell down a flight of stairs, I could call in sick to work (and life!), and someone else would take care of *me* for a while."

If you're nodding your head, and red as tomato soup about your responses, it's time to address what might be hijacking your moxie — and ultimately, your happiness — and causing you, from time to time, if not more regularly, to be a meanie to others. It's likely your boundaries — or lack thereof.

How Boundaries Amplify Moxie
(and Empower Leadership)

While writing this chapter, I typed the word *boundaries* into a search engine. I had to pick my jaw off my knees, or at the very least my clavicle, when I saw that it produced 319 million results.

Even more shocking, doing the same thing on Amazon.com produced 49,676 book recommendations. From how to set boundaries at work, when dating, in marriage, with kids and even in-laws, to how to set boundaries in therapeutic work with clients, and even how to set boundaries when songwriting, it's clear people are really looking for support in the boundary department — in all spheres of life. Particularly women. Most of the books and resources that popped up were written for a female audience. And while boundaries might sound super self-helpy and woo, they are intimately related to our ability to speak the truth to ourselves — and then boldly and compassionately communicate to others what we know we want, need, and deserve. Boundaries redirect us away from using our lives to advance other people's agendas and toward putting our own issues, causes, and passions smack-dab in the center of what we say and do.

One of my mentors once told me, in regard to youth facilitation, that "structure sets creativity free." She meant that if you want people (and this applies to those of us tweezing our grays and not just to gangly, pepperoni-faced preteens) to understand what's being asked of them, feel safe to say what's really on their minds, take risks in their conversations with each other, and play fully in the activities you lead, you need to provide rules. Then they'll be able to brainstorm. Be zany. Be unorthodox. For they will understand how success and failure will be measured. Otherwise, it's like herding cats to a museum.

Boundaries empower you to wake up each day clear on where you are headed. They shape how you make decisions and what you say to yourself and others, so you can stay in your lane rather than merge into everyone else's. Without them, you will find yourself guessing at the rules, constantly feeling like you are out of step with your true self and others, and ping-ponging between hustling for others' approval (a.k.a. the bunny stuff) and pushing through a persistent drizzle of pissiness (dragonosis) because you feel like you are a pawn in others' clumsy, painful, at times self-aggrandizing games. Most of us delude ourselves about our boundaries. Not sure if I'm talking about you? Then kindly answer the following: How are you feeling? How able are you, day to day, to step into your moxie? What kind of communication is coming from you — internally and externally?

A few years ago, one of the women in my speakers' mastermind created an assessment and asked some of the women in our group for feedback before releasing it. Typical group responses included, "The work you are doing is so needed." "I wish I knew you when…" "Oh, yeah, that used to be me. I'm glad I'm over those kinds of habits." As you probably surmised, the focus of the assessment was on creating and upholding boundaries. And the irony is that many of the women who professed to have mastered the art of getting their needs met and not overgiving, well, they showed up to their private coaching sessions complaining about clients and colleagues who were overstepping and making unreasonable requests. They repeatedly shared that they felt frustrated, ornery, depleted, and in the case of one woman, were considering a new business because the energetic cost of client work was no longer worth the revenue.

As a recovering overgiver, I am still a work in progress when it comes to upholding and articulating my boundaries. It's challenging for me to go more than a month without responding to email over the weekend. When I tell clients that they are looking to me for support I'm neither contracted nor trained to give, I feel like a supervisor who has just told a team member, "Your services are no longer needed here." Often, amid the struggle between upholding my boundaries and pleasing my peeps, I hop back and forth between bunny and dragon behavior. Cheetah whaaaaat?

I can still recall a Friday afternoon, not so long ago, when I received twelve or thirteen emails from the same three clients while I was on the road with spotty internet access. One moment I kowtowed. I started emailing people back as quickly as possible from my phone, terrified of what would happen if, God forbid, I waited until Monday when I had a decent internet connection and could use a proper computer (and write with more than my thumbs) to give them feedback on their keynotes. And then moments later, I was dropping f-bombs about the same clients' entitlement and bemoaning the fact that I don't charge enough.

While I'd like to think that if a friend or colleague gave me an assessment on my boundaries I would say, "I still have work to do in this area," realistically I'd probably answer, like many of my clients did, "Thank goodness I'm on the other side of that stuff." But I'm not. Most of us are not. I don't know an ambitious, high-performing, heart-centered woman who doesn't experience a certain amount of exhaustion tied not only to the quantity of her work but also to how she is performing it. To how she is allowing her desire to serve through her work, her community, and her family to wreak at least a bit of havoc on her self-care. Or lack thereof.

We cannot sustain the fullest expression of our moxie and leadership skills if we do not radically transform the way we are working. If we do not create, articulate, and rearticulate (again and again) our boundaries when other people, who are likely struggling in this area as well, inadvertently push us to work in a way that chips away at our energy, our gifts, and our overall life satisfaction. When we show the people we serve (our colleagues, clients, partners, children) that we are committed to transforming our own relationship with our work, we give them permission to transform the way they are working and showing up in their lives.

The world needs women who operate from their full potential. And women like Susan B. Anthony (who wasn't perfect but was steadfast in her dedication to opening up opportunities previously inaccessible to women) would be heartsick to know that too many women are failing to advocate for themselves. Are shouldering too much responsibility. Are swallowing heaps of desire. Are often out of community with other women. And consequently are a setback (or a shot of java) away from total collapse. Too many of us are not only failing to champion ourselves, but we're also failing to champion other women, as well as the issues and causes that need our engagement. We are not making it a priority to use our influence to reshape power structures, policies, and practices that are hurting women, children, and men. We are sitting on the sidelines as political, economic, social, and environmental advances lay on the cusp of erosion whenever there is an election and the new guard doesn't represent our interests. Or, when we do engage, we are comparing, complaining, or critiquing rather than harnessing our moxie to bring people together to solve issues that impact all of us — even those who don't see them through the same lens that we do.

My hope is that you will take a stand and ask for (nay, compassionately demand!) what you need to do your best work — and that you do it from a place of moxie. You will prioritize breath over busyness. You will proactively (and as necessary, retroactively) communicate this to the people you work, play, and live with. I hope that you will move your own creative work, dreams, and the issues that keep you up at night from the bottom of your to-do list to the top (or at least to the middle third). And that you will look to where you might be trespassing on other people's boundaries. We've all got to practice what we preach, and not ask of others, particularly women, what we would never ask of a man in the same position.

Boundary Proofing 101

As you know from earlier chapters, one of my foundational communication principles is that stepping into your moxie need not be complicated and that it should be fun — even when sensation is involved. Therefore, it requires a little structure, a lot of presence, and a yummy helping of intuition to navigate through inevitable moment-to-moment uncertainty. The same goes for boundaries. Think about what you need to be able to wake up every day, walk into any room, and participate in any conversation. To be able to say what you want to say, be who you want to be, and do it knowing that you belong, that what you say matters, that you are inherently imperfect, and that you are worthy of a great life and buckets of happiness anyway. Don't overcomplicate this with flashy formulas you can't remember and matching excuses for why you are playing at half your potential and why you hate the world and your role in it.

I need five things (really, it comes down to just five) to be in my moxie — and be a messenger of moxie for others.

1. Eight hours of sleep
2. To believe that I have the time I need to do everything I want to do (how much time I actually have is irrelevant; I only need to feel that it's abundant)
3. Financial freedom (by which I mean the ability to stop any facet of my work that isn't working for me if and when I choose)
4. Quality time with my loved ones
5. Quality time away from my loved ones — and alone with myself

I create and for the most part articulate and uphold a number of boundaries in order to facilitate things one through five. For example, for number one, I stop looking at my phone and computer at least an hour before I want to go to sleep, and I silence it at this time too. Otherwise, I'm tempted to pick it up if I hear a call or text. For number two, I schedule myself for twice as long as I think it will take me to accomplish most tasks I'm working on. For number three, I live in a starter home the size of many of my friends' master closets so that I can be in my power with my clients and tell them what I want to say without fear that if we go our separate ways I won't be able to pay my mortgage. (I want you to know that for a long time, I did not feel anything resembling financially free, and this is one I still struggle with as my business expenses run laps around my personal ones.) For number four, I strive not to respond to emails on weekends, and I keep Fridays client-free (so I can enter the weekend thinking about my family versus someone else's). And for number five, I periodically schedule time away from my kiddo and her daddy so that when I'm with them I remember how much they light me up — instead of deplete me. And so I don't default into pretending I'm having "tummy issues" and sneak away to the bathroom to read magazines and unwind. If you're a parent, I *know* you know what I'm talking about.

How about you? What are your moxie nonnegotiables? Do you have boundaries in place to safeguard them? What happens when you fail to articulate and uphold your boundaries? If you're anything like me, when boundaries are nonexistent, weak, or more secretive than the CIA, you devolve into feeling like a hot mess. Now, messiness is necessary from time to time, even for those of us who are (or at least like to moonlight as) clean freaks. Knowing we need a boundary, even if in the moment having one feels like wishful thinking, can help us make big, important pivots. For example, in the decision for my husband to join *my* (now *our*) business full-time, boundaries (or my growing lack of them) played a prominent role. With a partner gone most work weeks, it became close to impossible to enjoy quality family time and eke out much, if any, time for myself.

It's equally mess inducing when we fail to let other people in on our boundaries. Or, as I've been apt to do, fail to tell people who know our boundaries if and when they are acting like one of those cats herded to the museum. When we stay mum while feeling like a piece of expensive art on the wall and someone, say our boss or a client, is using us as his or her scratching pad. Telling someone about your boundary — that you have one, or that it's being trespassed — is simply another form of having a daring conversation. It may feel safer to throw on some flannel pajamas and take a siesta under the covers. Or volley between "Sure, no problem. I'd love to. Yes, yes, yes." And then, scream (at least in your head), *You ingrate — I wish you'd [have fun filling in this blank]*. Either way, it's close to impossible to be in your moxie — not to mention to be healthy, energized, pleasant, and socially engaged — until you consistently and compassionately speak your boundaries to yourself and others.

HEY, BOUNDARY!

You're a self-aware lady (or lad), so I'm confident that as you cruised through this chapter you spotted busted boundaries of yours left, right, and diagonally. In this Moxie Moment, I'm sharing with you an exercise I've cultivated to repair and rearticulate boundaries, my own and others'.

Directions: Please answer the following questions to (re)create your most pressing boundary, and then share it with the relevant people in your life. (If you prefer to do this in a worksheet, you may visit AlexiaVernon.com/MoxieBook to download a digital template.) Please use the proceeding hypothetical example as inspiration (and permission) to say what you know, at your core, you are aching to say.

1. In what area of your life are you not showing up from a place of moxie?
2. What boundary needs to be created (or reaffirmed) for you to show up, and speak up, with more moxie, grace, and ease?
3. Who do you need to communicate this boundary to?
4. How can you articulate the boundary with moxie?

Here are some tips for answering number 4: Speak the boundary as a statement of fact (versus as a question), say it with confidence (rather than as an apology), and make clear (and with compassion — for yourself and others) how you will uphold it.

Sample Responses

1. In what area of your life are you not showing up from a place of moxie? *Client communication.*
2. What boundary needs to be created (or reaffirmed) for you to show up, and speak up, with more moxie, grace, and ease? *I need my clients to stop text messaging me, especially over the weekends.*
3. Who do you need to communicate this boundary to? *Each of my ten retainer clients.*
4. How can you articulate the boundary with moxie? *Hey, client, I know my cell phone number is on my business card.*

And during the workweek, between nine and five, it's totally cool, if I'm not at my desk, to try my cell phone number. If you do call it, and I don't pick up, please leave a voicemail or send an email. I prefer to use text messaging only with family and friends. Thanks for your understanding.

QUESTIONS FOR REFLECTION

- What will be the payoff for communicating the boundary above (and other boundaries for which you use this process)?
- What's it costing you not to set or uphold your boundaries through your communication — or to second-guess the boundaries you have?
- How might your moxie (as it pertains to boundaries) empower the people in your life to define, communicate, and maintain their boundaries as well?
- As you make a habit of creating and maintaining your boundaries, how does your perception of your moxie, your energy, and your overall personal and professional satisfaction evolve?

Again, don't, pretty please, overcomplicate (re)articulating your boundaries. Resist going bunny by apologizing for what you want and need or by overexplaining your boundaries. You don't have to pretend to be always misplacing your phone to explain why you aren't answering client text messages. You don't have to purposefully drop your phone into the toilet to buy yourself a few days off the grid. And don't set yourself up for dragon-outburst moments by failing to ask boundary trespassers to step back. Even if they should know better, the people in our professional and personal lives often need reminders. When it comes to boundaries, get clear on what you need, forgive yourself and whomever you are about to speak to for his or her role in how you are feeling, say what you want to say, and then put a period on it. Redirect your attention toward what you want to create more of, instead of rehashing what's been lacking and unintentionally creating more of it.

By the time I performed my senior-year history-class monologue, I had a deep, deep love for Tracy Chapman — because of her social activism and powerful music, and for waking me up to the privilege of my race and class. This presentation became one of my favorite school projects. Leading up to it, I listened to Chapman's lyrics over and over again, and I like to believe they worked their way into my soul and became imprinted in my cells. Nary a week goes by that I don't still catch myself humming her song "Fast Car": "I had a feeling I belonged. I had a feeling I could be someone. Be someone. Be someone." When I first heard those words, they were aspirational for me. Fortunately, more days than not, I now feel like I am the hero I once was waiting for. I consistently choose the role of protagonist in the stories I tell about myself. I speak up for what I want — and almost as often, for what I refuse to tolerate, and I strive to do it kindly. And I want that for *you*. Little did I know, a bit more than half a lifetime ago, that the assignment that initially felt like such a letdown was actually a wake-up call. It would illuminate the very thing I'd dedicate my life to — creating a pathway for other women to feel like they belong. So *you* could know, with absolute certainty, that you can go out into the world, speak up, and be someone too — the most authentic, vulnerable, tender, and fierce version of yourself.

Twenty-first-century life is wildly more complicated than when Susan B. Anthony roamed the streets of Rochester, New York, one hundredish years ago. And no matter how much moxie you step into, there are going to be episodes, months, years, seasons that challenge the crap (and at times, the soul) out of you. In the next chapter, I'll tell you about one of my episodes, and why, even when it feels as if the universe is throwing you constraints rather than cosmic winks, everything is always happening *for* you. Everything can enhance, rather than diminish, your moxie...if you allow it to.

12

WHEN THE UNIVERSE BITES YOUR BUM-BUM, DON'T LET HER STEAL YOUR VOICE

You may write me down in history
With your bitter, twisted lies,
You may tread me in the very dirt
But still, like dust, I'll rise.

— MAYA ANGELOU

I loved being pregnant. I was like one of those pregnant ladies you see pictured in women's magazines whom you curse at and say, "That girl must have been airbrushed. She can't possibly glow like that at eight months pregnant." While at the same time a part of you is thinking, "But what if she *is* that happy? Why can't I have that too?"

Even though I gained fifty pounds during my pregnancy, I loved it. It all went to my belly — and my boobs! (D-size breasts after a lifetime of little As — smokin'!) I was doing downward dogs up until seventy-two hours before I gave birth. And during most of my pregnancy, I was really enjoying the second career I had given myself, which was preparing for natural childbirth. Steve and I were practicing our hypnobirthing exercises each day to handle the pain of labor and delivery, and we had curated the perfect mixes of essential oils and songs to augment the delivery experience.

And then, when I was a few days post-term, Steve and I learned that our baby girl wasn't breathing quite right. And things, well, they went way off my seven-page birth plan. I was immediately admitted to the hospital, and labor was induced. Bed rest. Oxygen mask. Cervical ripening. Pitocin. Ruptured membranes. Water broken. And finally, I submitted to the epidural I vowed I would never choose. Everything I did not want for myself and my baby became my birth story. But when my daughter entered the world a day and a half later, healthy, able to breathe once her umbilical cord was no longer wrapped around her neck, and was placed on my chest, I thought the worst was behind me.

Let the mommy-and-me yoga begin.

This probably doesn't come as much of a surprise, but I never made it to one of those classes.

Although from day one my daughter would sleep in three-to-four-hour stretches, and by six weeks was actually sleeping through the night, during my first ninety days as a new mom I never slept more than two hours in a twenty-four-hour period. The day we came home as a family from the hospital, the cat I'd had since I was nineteen years old passed away — loudly, painfully, without the dignity his life warranted, as I nursed my daughter in my arms. And from that day on, my daughter never nursed again. I pumped, I saw a lactation consultant, I pushed through multiple rounds of clogged milk ducts and infections, but I wasn't the same. The joy of new motherhood was quickly and completely eclipsed by my grief. The depression that set in after the death of our cat quickly morphed into anger (this was so *not* the birth story I had written and memorized) and then into anxiety, which consumed me from the moment I opened my eyes until the moment they closed each day — however brief a period that was.

Not only could I not sleep, I also couldn't eat. I couldn't change a diaper or get my daughter in and out of a car seat without help. I worried about my daughter getting sick. I worried about my getting sick. I stopped leaving the house, for fear, after I did get sick, that I'd get sick all over again. And one night, after a terrifying nightmare in which I saw men shrouded in white sheets stabbing me as they attempted to steal my baby, I rolled out of bed and onto the ground, and was pretty sure I was never going to get up again. The chasm between pregnant me and postpartum me couldn't have been vaster.

Throughout my journey into the bowels of postpartum depression (PPD), I flogged myself with questions like, *Who are you, Lady Privilege, to be blubbering about the difficulties of new motherhood? Clean the snot off your face and go love up on your kid.* And in the moments when all my sass and snark were gone, which were most, I asked myself, *How can I dedicate my life to empowering the voices of others when motherhood has so totally disconnected me from my own voice? How can I facilitate breakthroughs for others when I am breaking down so completely myself?* Maybe you too have felt this dichotomy and have wondered during a difficult episode or season of life, *How can I profess to do _____ for others when I'm such a Pitiable Posey in my own life right now?!*

While I'll never know exactly what triggered my PPD, or what specifically pulled me out (for within a week of starting a daily cocktail of natural progesterone, antidepressant, and sleeping pill I felt fully myself again), what I do know, with absolute certainty, is that this difficult chapter in my life ushered in a new era for my moxie. After I recalibrated, I felt emboldened to take even greater risks in my speaking and with my business. Losing my voice and hitting my perception of my personal rock bottom shook loose any last crumbs of self-doubt (for I survived an identity squall and now knew I could survive *anything*). And I had a sense that if I stepped even more deeply into my moxie — released any remaining vestiges of my people-pleasing habit, completely stopped defining my self-worth by my client list or revenue, and never again sanitized my words or my message to protect others — I just might achieve a level of success and purposefulness I had not given myself permission to fully envision or experience.

As I would soon learn, I was spot-on in my assessment. For in my four and a half years, post–postpartum depression, I have busted some big moves in my life and work. And while not everything in my life has been easy-peasy, I have simultaneously heightened my ability to see the people I support on their leadership and speaking journeys with more compassion and empathy, and I have harnessed buckets of joy through serving them.

Everything Is Happening *for* You

While I loved everything about Ariel in *The Little Mermaid* as a Hypercolor T-shirt-wearing, zitty tween, almost three decades later I now think she may be one of the most antiquated of Disney heroines, and I consider her deeply damaging to young women's vocal development. Okay, she's not Aurora-from-*Sleeping-Beauty* bad — she does more than look pretty and sleep — but she's not far behind. I mean, Ariel decided to trade in her voice for a shot with a dude she barely knew — with less thought than it takes me to choose between a glass of Cabernet or Malbec with a spaghetti dinner. And I *always* pick the Cab, so that's saying something.

While I fortunately have never sacrificed my voice for a guy (and I'm grateful every day that the universe threw me a super juicy bone by sending me Steve so early in life), I do think that I went Ariel, in my own way, for so many years because I erroneously and unconsciously carried around the belief that either I could have my voice or I could be happy. And my self-talk and behavior indicated that I was choosing the latter, while I felt anything but. By the time I was preggers, however, I knew that I had concocted a lie. I had reprogrammed my head, heart, and voice for moxie, and I had made a business out of showing other people how to tell their truths onstage, at work, and in life. I had a voice, I used it every day, and I was happier than a prom queen at her high school reunion.

And yet somehow in between getting strapped into a bed for a medicalized childbirth I did not want and hitting my bedroom floor face-first less than ninety days postpartum, I felt like I had reversed hundreds of paces and was again trading in my voice (and my happiness), this time for a supposedly normal rite of passage called motherhood. Previously I had thought that the circuitous path to trusting and reclaiming my voice after head gear and sexual abuse was tough — but this motherhood stuff, it was gutting me in new, never-again-do-I-want-to-experience-this ways. I loved my child...but I loved myself with a child in my belly, versus in the world, even more. I knew to say such a thing out loud would make me a vile human being to most people in my life, and while I didn't know if I always would feel that way (and fortunately I did not, *do not*), in my initial days postpartum I felt like a rat in a glue trap — which is to say, thoroughly stuck and within inches of my life.

And that's the beauty, always in hindsight, of these moments that split us open and force us to question everything we think we know about ourselves. They are happening *for* us. For *you*. It's not the Big G, the universe, or past-life karma punishing or seeking to scar you. It's a cosmic wink from somewhere, you choose the sender, lovingly awakening you to know yourself, and to speak up for yourself even more expressively. Your ability to rise when confronted with setbacks — both those you willingly tumbled right into and those that showed up like a Halloween-night house egging, meaning, through no fault of your own — is one of the most important moxie muscles you can flex. If you are serious about pairing heart-centered, high-impact self-talk with equally kind and effective communication and leadership in the world, harness the learning of your bum-bum-biting moments and accept their invitation into more moxie.

Don't Quit: Reset and Recalibrate

We are inundated with stories of celebrities whose failures and traumas have been training ground for the resilience needed to ultimately create epic achievements for themselves and others. Oprah Winfrey, for example, suffered physical and sexual childhood abuse, was a runaway, pregnant, and lost a baby by fourteen, and failed early in her career as a primetime news coanchor. J.K. Rowling was a depressed, jobless single mother living from one unemployment check to the next before a publisher finally picked up *Harry Potter and the Sorcerer's Stone* and jump-started Rowling's transformation into one of the world's bestselling authors of all time. And one of my favorite perseverance stories is that of Elon Musk. While you likely know Musk for his many accomplishments, including serving as the cofounder and current CEO of Tesla, you may not know that his pathway to revolutionizing electric vehicles was anything but linear. Earlier in his life, Musk was ousted from PayPal, where he was CEO. He nearly died from cerebral malaria while on a vacation in his native South Africa. He lost a son to SIDS. He almost went bankrupt from three failed SpaceX launches, and then he ultimately poured his entire life savings into Tesla when it too almost brought him back to the brink of bankruptcy. Yet if many of us were to experience even a fraction of the setbacks many of our greatest trailblazers have endured, we would feel like we were permanently marooned on an island of failure and tragedy.

For the first half of my life I had zero distress tolerance and resiliency. In middle school, when I wasn't cast as Clara in *The Nutcracker* ballet, I quit my dance school and released my dream of being a professional ballet dancer. Yup, I literally gave up a full-merit scholarship to a dance academy because I was so ticked off that I got cast as a mouse rather than as the starring ingenue. (Even though I had played the role of Clara at another ballet school two years earlier!) My capacity to rally amid setbacks, disappointment, and discomfort diminished as I moved through school. In high school, when my roommate in a summer college immersion program smoked pot in our dorm room the first day of our classes, I was so terrified I'd get arrested and never be able to go to college (or have the option to run for public office) that I called my parents and told them I wanted to leave. I did the same thing a year later when I was a college freshman — withdrawing from the first university I attended after the first day. Of orientation. This time I didn't even make it to class, I was *that* uncomfortable (and underwhelmed) after my first keg party.

I used to think that a key indicator of success and self-growth was one's ability to get knocked down and immediately get back up again. Now I know that resilience is much more than the ability to suck up a certain amount of discomfort — something I'm still working on. (I'm pretty sure if someone had told me I could quit motherhood during my first ninety days, I would have.) These days I measure my resilience by my ability to take setbacks, especially those I could not plan for, like a painful backhand to the cheek. (And please know that the only person who has backhanded me, accidentally, she says, is my preschooler. At least half a dozen times — so I know this feeling excruciatingly well.)

Resilience isn't running away from your child, or pretending your cheek isn't burning like mad. It's being able to feel the sting fully, and more important, receive the lesson from it (that lesson being, in my case, that when your child is dancing like a lunatic with her shirt over her head, get the heck out of the way before your face gets mistaken for a throw pillow). But seriously, when you are stepping into your moxie, doing more, risking more, and readying yourself for contributing more, the smackdowns are often much harder — yet, on the other side of recovery, the discoveries, if you don't run from them, are all the more glorious.

Now, when I suggested earlier in the chapter that the past few years have been amazeballs, I do not want you to think that there have not still been a crap-ton of nauseatingly stinky, manure-filled moments. I simply experience them differently — and as a result, most become doorways into deep transformation. About a year prior to writing this chapter, I prepared for what I had determined would be a wildly successful online launch of one of my speaker training programs. I did all the right things. I ran an ambitious Facebook ad campaign to generate several thousand new leads. I lined up affiliates who shared my work with their audiences. I had my sales page and marketing emails created almost a month before I needed them. You would have thought I was a hoarder in remission given the boxes — So. Many. Boxes. — that I cleared from my home office to cleanse stagnant chi. (It's okay, you can roll your eyes. I would.) And I told Steve, "When we hit or exceed [I was a cocky little baller] our goals, we'll be set up for you to leave your job and join me full-time in the business in six months."

This wasn't just posturing, I assure you. I felt at the depth of my being that this would be my most successful program launch yet. I set my early-bird (which means my first-forty-eight-hours) sales goals, and...I was two-thirds *under* them when the promotional period ended. Even though no launch is over until the cart closes (and for those who have ever been in a marketer's launch funnel, you know that even when enrollment ends there's usually still one "final-call" email), I knew that I was not going to come anywhere near my financial goal. Steve would not be joining the business. Simultaneously, during the first few days of my launch, as I grew a worry bubble bigger than the lung it surely was pushing against, Steve learned that after nearly a year of not having to travel for his work, he would now be required to work every single Monday to Friday (and sometimes Saturday) in another state. Had I been within sniffing distance of my financial goal, Steve could have said "peace out" to his employer and joined me a bit earlier than I'd fantasized — but of course, that was not to be.

Now, here's why I love this story so much. After two to three days of sloppy boo-hoo-hooing, during which I granted myself permission to feel fully *everything* I was feeling, I evicted myself from my pity party. I said to God, "I'm super bummed I called this one as wrong as pollsters called the 2016 presidential election, but I'm on the lookout for the message you want me to receive." And I meant it. I did the wildly uncomfortable, at times totally nonintuitive, work I'm about to invite you to do during your own the-universe-is-biting-my-bum-bum moments. Spoiler alert: Within six months of this disappointing series of events, I earned more than I'd earned the entire year before. As a result, Steve was able to leave his job and join me full-time in the business. And I scored an amazing literary agent and signed both a traditional print and an audio book deal for the book that you are reading (or listening to).

How did I reset and recalibrate? Sheesh, it was so simple. And yet not easy. So. Not. Easy. But simple. And it truly expanded my capacity to be with instead of unravel from situational distress. My process included first asking God [insert whatever word works for you here] this question, without attachment to the answer:

What would you have me learn?

And I asked that question every single day, repeatedly. In morning meditation, as soon as my alarm went off. While driving to a meeting or to the grocery store. During my daughter's TV hour (because remember, I was now a single mom during the workweek so there wasn't a lot of free time for mindfulness). And always before I closed my eyes at night. Each day, I kept asking the question, with the commitment of an addict on the prowl for her next fix. And when I felt myself trying to force an answer, which happened quite a bit, I put my attention elsewhere so I could allow the divine to speak what I needed to discover — even if it wasn't on my desired timeline.

Second, I told myself my Hollywood story. I bet you have one of those — a version of your life that Hollywood would deem blockbuster worthy. When I visualize my movie, I like to go straight to a climactic moment. When Anne Hathaway (playing me) has her big breakdown (probably with much better hair and waterproof mascara). During the bungled launch scene, I determined the voiceover I wanted spoken when Anne cries, "And that was the moment I realized I could make it as a mother on my own." (More on how I realized this was the needed voiceover in a moment.)

And third, I procured evidence, quickly, that proved I was a successful person. While free time was scarce, with my hubs out of state, during the months he was away I committed one hour a day (usually after I put my daughter to bed), and whenever I awoke during the night and my mind went all whirling dervish, to work on the proposal for this book. My first-quarter-of-the-year goal — finish my book proposal. My second-quarter goal — pitch proposal to agents. Notice, my goal wasn't *get* an agent. Or *get* a book deal.

For those goals were outside my control and, I knew, could chip away at my moxie if they didn't unfold on my timeline. But setting a goal that I was in complete control of achieving, and ultimately did achieve, ahead of schedule, helped me recalibrate big-time.

Collecting quick evidence of my successfulness was something I failed to do at the onset of postpartum depression. And once PPD had its tentacles around me, I couldn't think about success when my chances at survival felt on par with someone aboard the *Titanic* after hitting the iceberg — someone in steerage, to be clear. I'm pretty sure that feeling, so divorced from a recent success at one of the most vulnerable moments of my life, is also one of the reasons that my self-worth plummeted from what felt like ten thousand feet in the sky to ten thousand feet underground within a few weeks. And, unfortunately, once a bum-bum-biting moment attacks your sense of worthiness, it's tough to stop yourself from sliding down into deeper self-loathing — let alone cultivate the faith and energy to recalibrate and move forward.

To recap, when it feels like a higher power is punishing you for what must have been some truly heinous acts you committed in a former life, to practice resilience so that you can step back into your moxie, I recommend putting into practice the following three steps.

1. Ask God, the divine, or the universe (whatever title works best for you) to illuminate the lesson you're supposed to learn. As you ask, commit to unhooking completely from any timeline during which you expect to see an answer.
2. Deploy the Hollywood voiceover strategy to trick yourself into choosing empowering self-talk.
3. Finally, remind yourself that you are wired for success by pursuing a quick win (one in which success is measured by doing your work and not by an outside variable you can't control).

Now I want to share a bit more about a lesson I needed to learn after the disappointing launch. It still makes me weepy to remember how long it took me to learn it — for it was a lesson I had failed to learn three years earlier (and it therefore had shown up again).

I could (can) handle mothering. Alone.

A factor contributing to my postpartum depression, I realized in hindsight, was a limiting belief that I wasn't strong enough to take on all that's required to be a work-from-home mom — especially not without the full-time support of a spouse. (I fully surrendered to postpartum depression when my husband learned that in a few weeks he was going to be traveling for work a handful of days every month.) When God, or the universe, gives us an opportunity to cultivate an important mindset, heartset, and skillset, and we don't cultivate it, that opportunity will come back around — often at a super inconvenient moment, as it did for me.

While in my first days as a new mom I berated myself for not knowing how to extract milk from my breasts, work a convertible car seat, or keep my newborn in a swaddle, all those examples of my "failures as a mom" were actually masking a much bigger fear. Unconsciously, I had constructed the story that I couldn't finally go all in with my business (the desire it felt like I birthed at the exact same moment my daughter passed through me and into the world); scale this business I was building the way I craved (so that I could sustain my role as primary breadwinner and provide my family with the kind of financial freedom and opportunities my husband's sufficient but capped salary couldn't); and still be the kind of engaged, fully present mom I grew up with and also wanted to be (even with my husband gone a few days each week). First World problems, absolutely, but mine nonetheless.

Now, I don't want to suggest that Steve bailed on me or our

daughter whenever he worked out of town. His remote partnering and parenting were amazing. He called each day, never missed a weekend trip to the grocery store, and had a lot of impromptu weekend daddy-daughter dates so that I could have some extra work time. But, well, being at home with your young child five days a week, while trying to grow a company, it's a lot. And yet during the last six months before Steve joined what is now our business, when weekday single parenting became my norm, I did not go back into my postpartum story and unravel. I practiced the three strategies for cultivating resilience like my life depended on it (because I knew it did), and I crushed it. During this period, I created the most rapid business growth I ever had until that point. I simultaneously hit some major thought leadership milestones, and I released the last shackles of shame about my postpartum depression — because I finally understood that it, like every difficult episode we experience, had been there to teach me. I finally saw that painful chapter for the gift that it was. And the best part of this current period was that I felt really connected to the divine.

Now, I don't remember waking up one morning and saying, "Aha, that's what this all means! White-lady guilt be gone!" (And, being realistic, I'll never know, for sure, the true cause of my PPD, even if the lesson I learned in the aftermath felt like it was divinely sent for me.) My awareness emerged incrementally — in meditation, while cooking dinner, in the loo — like a whisper or gentle tickle from within. And when I got out of my own way and let go of trying to control forces outside myself, focused on buffing up my resilience muscles, and practiced the three strategies I previously described, I created the cash flow for Steve to join me as COO and released the story that I am uncomfortable being uncomfortable. And when Steve did join me full-time in the business (on the same date I fantasized he would during the disappointing launch earlier that year), I was ready, because I had done the deeper healing and expansion work I needed to do for our partnership in work and life to be an act of moxie (versus a bandage for my feelings of *I can't do this on my own anymore*).

The Gifts of Bum-Bum-Biting Moments

Resilience is defined both as "the capacity to recover quickly from difficulties" and as "the ability of a substance or object to spring back into shape." While I know through firsthand and client experience that you can be resilient even if you don't "recover quickly"— and actually, from a moxie perspective, I would measure success more by your ability to heal and expand in the face of difficulties than by the speed with which you can again pass as your normal self — I'm particularly fond of the second definition. I'm not sure about you, but I don't default to thinking about tough times as an inherent springboard back to my best self. Yet opportunities that cultivate our resilience can be such springboards for us — for you.

That is why embracing (versus taking cover from or bearing down on) your bum-bum-biting moments is one of your most direct pathways to stepping into your moxie. Because moxie is choosing to be brave, speaking up, and disrupting the status quo, I believe you actually need your bum-bum-biting moments to automatically (or at least, more frequently) choose moxie in the pedestrian moments that define your day-to-day. That bears repeating, so I'll say it again. You actually *need* bum-bum-biting moments in order to step into the fullest expression of your moxie. Here are some of the specific gifts you unwrap when you choose moxie during these episodes in your life.

Creativity

One of the top ways that resilience strengthens your moxie is by forcing you to tap into your creativity. For whatever has gotten you through similar episodes in your past is often not what gets you through your current situation. And that is precisely why the situation has shown up — for your evolution. Navigating through a bum-bum-biting moment can be a creative process, if you let it. Creativity can be finding that new, renegade way to solve your crisis, or it can be patching together resources when, at first glance, you deem them in short supply. You can also cultivate creativity by choosing to narrate your experience as a chapter about your highest learning and growth — rather than one about loss or failure.

Empathy

When you choose resilience and, as a by-product, moxie, you are also by default growing your capacity to empathize, which is a superpower when it comes to connecting with others, positioning yourself as someone who is relatable and trustworthy, and empowering other people to heal from their pain and be their best selves. When I read testimonials from my coaching program participants, I'm grateful to discover that many have commented on my ability to really see and be in their experiences with them. Now, if you are a therapist, undoubtedly that makes you want to cringe. And I assure you, I do not take on anybody else's "stuff" as my own — at least, not anymore. (Okay, sometimes I still do, but so much less than I used to.) For when you've lived through your own fair share of bum-bum-biting moments, it does grow your ability to empathize with others through their painful episodes and to more adeptly hold space for them as a result.

Transparency

Some people choose to be private about their bum-bum-biting moments, a practice that unfortunately usually breeds both secrecy and additional suffering for the bite-ee. However, those on the moxie path allow setbacks (irrespective of their magnitude) to heighten their truth telling — to themselves, first and foremost, and to others — professionally and personally. You cultivate transparency when you are honest about where and how you are hurting (especially when you aren't asking people to fix you and want them simply to hold space for your experience). And when you admit that you aren't perfect, that you don't have it all together, you also fortify yourself against perfectionism — and perfectionism must be slayed in order for moxie to thrive.

Receiving

When you unapologetically own that you cannot and therefore won't attempt to power through difficult times alone, you open yourself up to receive support — something that is hard for a lot of women to do (including the one who is typing this out for you). While many women may feel, and at times complain, that nobody takes care of us, the truth is that most of us aren't asking for the support we need on a regular basis. As a consequence, we are getting in the way of attracting, and when it's offered, accepting, other people's help. (Remember our discussion in the last chapter on articulating and upholding boundaries?) Bum-bum-biting moments are fertile ground for strengthening your capacity to ask for and receive support from the people in your life — mates, children, extended family, friends, colleagues, community members. And, when you practice asking the question, "What am I supposed to learn?" without secretly wishing for a quick answer, you also enhance your ability to receive divine guidance, which is, in my humble opinion, the greatest gift we can invite and accept into our lives.

Self-Awareness

Self-awareness is the ability to see the truth of ourselves — the good, the bad, and the truly baffling — with compassionate clarity. When you are self-aware, you squelch any and all desire to critique yourself for who you are (and who you are not...yet) and instead, you simply observe and appreciate who you are in the present moment. Resilience does this to you, for you. Because at its core, resilience, like forgiveness, is about making peace with *what is* rather than holding on to the hope of who you, others, or a situation could have been. As a by-product of resilience, self-awareness activates the fullest expression of your moxie. For when you learn to speak to yourself and others as you/they are, from a feeling of enoughness, your communication will flow clearly, easily, and compassionately.

Over the years some of my greatest discoveries about how to navigate through tough times have come from my clients — people, usually women, who find me because they want to turn their heartbreak into a harrowing, tour-de-force keynote or inspirational talk for others. Often these are women who have lost children or partners, or have suffered unspeakable abuse (often at the hands of those closest to them).

A huge part of resilience for these women was realizing that their survival and the lessons they have learned must be shared. This is a discovery I suspect you may have had as well — that what you have survived can provide inspiration, insight, and healing for others.

LET YOUR STORY TRANSFORM THE LIVES OF OTHERS

As you've made your way through this chapter, most likely you've replayed various bum-bum-biting moments from your life. As a result, you may have discovered lessons previously embedded deep within your suffering. Or even asked yourself, *How can I use what I've been through to be of greater service to others?* For this Moxie Moment exercise, there are no step-by-step instructions — simply an invitation to sit with the Questions for Reflection and let them illuminate how your bum-bum-biting moments can make a positive impact on others.

QUESTIONS FOR REFLECTION

- What are the top lessons you have learned from your bum-bum-biting life events? (Suggestion: if you are struggling to excavate lessons, consider going back to chapter 1 and doing the Five Rs Moxie Moment exercise with the memories that are coming up.)
- What people, communities, or groups can benefit from hearing you tell your story?
- How could sharing your story directly with someone in your life, or as a guest speaker for an audience you identified, allow you to step into your moxie, be of service, and develop your thought leadership?

In our final chapter together (sniffle, sniffle), we'll explore how to use your moxie mindset, heartset, and skillset to speak up and out about the issues that matter most to you — so that you can build the work, family, and community you want to be a part of. I'll give you an opportunity to think about the legacy you are leaving. Because you *are* leaving one, whether or not you are conscious of it. Together we'll explore how to ensure that the legacy you are forging through what you say and do, who you spend time with, and who and what you champion, is the one you want to be leaving.

13

CHOOSE LEGACY OVER FAME

My real dream is that everybody will see their self-interest tied up with someone else, whether or not they see them, and see that as an opportunity for growing closer together as a culture and as a world.

— MAJORA CARTER

If you had asked me, when I was a tween, "Alexia, what do you want to be when you grow up?" I would have told you, "A ballerina." Then I would have shut my mouth, self-consciously looked down at my Doc Martens, and mentally played out the full career trajectory I had developed for myself:

After my dancing career, I'm going to be an astronaut. And then, when I'm too old for that, I'm going to start my own school for girls. And then, I'm going to write a book about my life. I'll be interviewed by Larry King. Hollywood will make a movie about my life. I'll play myself, of course, and then I'll win an Oscar for my

harrowing performance. After that, I'll run for public office, proba-
bly president, and in my twilight years I'll start a nonprofit, funded
by all my famous friends, to help girls who've been sexually abused.

Fortunately, I was too emotional and empathetic to be labeled a narcissist, but I definitely had an unhealthy appetite for significance for a lot of years. My need to be seen as a hotshot greatly decreased by the time I left graduate school and could no longer use grades as a way to prove myself. I don't think I'll ever fully shed my enjoyment of outward approval, despite my longing to, but I now understand that many factors drive my desire for visibility, as they likely do yours. Not all are bad. With status can come great impact. However, you don't need to have millions of social media followers or a shiny trophy from your peers to speak up, address issues that matter to you, and leave a legacy you can be proud of. True influence comes from focusing on who you seek to serve, and the change you want to facilitate, rather than from thinking that once you have a sizable following, *then* you can be an agent of change. Whenever I have clients who complain about underearning, a lack of their own clients, or nonexistent media attention, I find that their yearning to be known often runs very deep. As a result, they unknowingly put more attention on positioning themselves within their industry than on doing the important work and making the impact they profess they want to have.

I've had the privilege of coaching a lot of leaders who have used their power to address injustices and positively affect people's lives. Whether they were leading companies or social movements, not one of these leaders has ever shared it was her desire for accolades that prompted her to take action. Each spoke up and led in order to serve the people she cared about and to effect lasting change. Her passion became contagious, resulting in her mobilizing an audience far greater than she ever imagined possible. And with more followers and proselytizers her influence — and as a result, her salary and title — organically grew.

Speak Your Truth as an Act of Service

I always snicker when I read books telling smart, driven women how to "get involved." You know what you care about, what breaks (and opens) your heart, and what more than likely keeps showing up for you — because it's nudging you to take action. Whether what tugs at you is child abuse, racism, genocide, gun violence, refugees, chemicals in our water supply, the opioid crisis, mental illness, or mean people in your workplace, think about what a first step might look like that allows you to begin right where you are. Perhaps it's proposing a new policy at work, or if you are an entrepreneur, giving a portion of your revenue to a charitable organization. Maybe it's lending your voice to an effort already under way in your community, auditioning for a local speaking event so that you can tell your story and give visibility to an important humanitarian issue, or speaking up to those closest to you when they fail to mask their prejudice behind comments like "those people." Don't make it complicated, but also, don't be complicit in maintaining the status quo. I didn't write this book for you to step into your moxie for your own gain. #SorryNotSorry. I did it so you can use you voice and influence to champion the many issues and causes that require your dang championship.

Once you begin to speak (and act) up — whether it's through having interpersonal conversations, bringing your coworkers together, writing a blog post, or conducting media interviews, consider how you can enroll others in your vision. When I think back to the first quarter of my life, and my obnoxious infatuation with fame (which often ran parallel to my equally strong desire not to speak up and make a fool of myself), at least one limiting belief that motivated my hustle for awards, titles, and press was the idea that great leaders are those who *start* things. When in reality, great leaders are those who *grow* things. And the only way to grow anything is by allowing it to expand beyond you.

Now, I understand where my insecurity and scarcity mentality came from, why I felt like I had to be a lone ranger and make everything I wanted happen by myself and be celebrated for it. When you don't see a lot of women in leadership roles, it creates an environment in which you feel you have to compete with the women around you to claim the spotlight. It also explains why, when a woman makes a mistake, misuses her power, or fails to champion other women, it's often other women who are first in line to tear her down — rather than offer her constructive feedback. Have you noticed that guys aren't so bloody hard on each other? They see other dudes making bank, starting companies, winning awards, inventing doohickeys, whatever it is, and they don't act as though there is only one opportunity for success, and if they don't get it they'll be relegated to a lifetime of obscurity. They don't go all mean-guy on one another. Rather, they are emboldened by one another. They believe there are more than enough seats at the table for everyone who shows up. Ladies, when we see other women busting big moves in the world, we need to help our sistas out — promote their work, fund their work, celebrate their achievements. We need to tell ourselves, and truly believe, *If she can do it, so can I!* And if we do find from time to time that all the seats at a table are taken, or that we don't like the culture of the table we're sitting at, then we can go sit at a new one — and invite other women (and men) whose values align with ours to join us at it.

A core tenet of stepping into your moxie is letting your voice be heard. Another is knowing when to step up and when to step back. When to listen and when to speak, ask questions, or give other women (and men) without the privileges you may have been afforded an opportunity at the mic — so that your words and actions lead to positive and lasting change. The world needs more female leaders, and I want you to be one of them. If you are gunning to be a figurehead — a CEO, an executive director, an elected leader — take some time to discern where your motivation stems from. If ego eclipses service, self-correct. Then get back on that leadership bullet train, keep your eye on the impact you seek, ensure you are empowering the voices of others to speak for themselves, and resist the urge to be known for your acts of moxie.

Leadership can mean starting something, and it can also be contributing your voice, time, and energy to somebody else's initiative in order to expand its reach. I've often thought it would be interesting to grant investment dollars to leaders who join (versus create) start-ups, social enterprises, and movements in order to increase their reach. Leadership can also mean beginning from where you are, laying the tracks for progress, and then handing over your idea, project, or business to someone who can take it to the next level. When you lead from a place of moxie, you focus on the impact of your work — even when, especially when, what you catalyze grows beyond you.

In a *New York Times* interview, #MeToo movement founder Tarana Burke was asked how she felt about her words *Me Too* being used to spawn the movement — a movement that, in its early days, was not connected to her. At the time, few knew that Burke, an African American woman, first spoke the now infamous phrase in 2006 to illuminate that survivors of sexual abuse, assault, exploitation, and harassment in racially diverse communities lack access to rape crisis centers and counseling. Burke would have been fully justified to express frustration about *Me Too* moving away from its African American activist roots or for initially not being acknowledged for her contribution, but she didn't do that. I love Burke's response in this interview, as it demonstrates exactly what it means to be a leader who puts impact first. "I think it is selfish for me to try to frame Me Too as something that I own. It is bigger than me.... This is about survivors."

Diana Simone is another example of a woman who led from where she was, without self-interest. A massage therapist from Fort Worth, Texas, Simone was devastated when, in 1996, nine-year-old Amber Hagerman from neighboring Arlington, Texas, was abducted and later found dead — less than five miles from where she had been taken. As she watched the media coverage of this tragedy, Simone couldn't help but wonder if a community alert could be issued when children go missing — to help communities come together during the initial hours when it might still be possible to bring children home safely to their families. Without knowing what such an alert would look like, or how it would be sounded, Diana called a local Dallas–Fort Worth radio station and shared the seeds of her idea. Within a year, seven local (and competing!) radio station managers collaborated to set up a local broadcast alert system, based on her initial musings. Today, America's Missing: Broadcast Emergency Response (known as the AMBER Alert) is shared through all major media distribution channels. And over the past twenty years, similar systems have spread throughout the world. Simone and I spoke at the same TEDxWomen event, and in her talk she shared that the AMBER Alert has reunited 881 abducted children (and counting) with their families. While Simone may never be a household name, what influence she has had — and what a legacy she will leave behind.

There are myriad ways to use your voice, step into your moxie, and create lasting impact. Have you ever taken the time to really think about what you want *your* legacy to be? Once you know the footprints you want to leave behind at your organization, in your family, and for your community, you can direct your efforts accordingly and more purposefully use your voice. I used to erroneously believe that legacy was a privilege reserved for those whose contributions made it into history books or for supremely wealthy folks who left bajillions of dollars to their foundations or families. Yes, fame and fortune can aid you in your change making — as can setting a clear intention and acting on it. You can speak up locally, as a concerned citizen. You can also show up to your job, to your business, and to the people who matter most to you, committed to using your voice to build the future you want for you, for others, and for generations to come.

LEGACY VISUALIZATION

Directions: Complete the following visualization at a time when, and in a place where, you can have quiet, peace, and presence. Once you get there, read the following script. (Note: if you prefer to complete this Moxie Moment through an extended guided visualization, which I recommend, you may listen to the audio I've created for you at AlexiaVernon.com/MoxieBook.)

Imagine you are at the end of your career. You are being honored by a community of your peers for outstanding service. You are sitting in the front row of a theater, auditorium, or stadium. Take in the splendor of the space. See the stage. Feel the presence of the people sitting in the audience who have gathered to celebrate your influence.

A mentor of yours, somebody who has believed in you, supported you, and championed you, is about to introduce you before you accept your award. Listen to the words this person speaks. She or he is sharing how your life and work have had a positive impact on others. Take a few moments to let those words sink in. To imprint in your memory, and your soul.

Now time-travel back, halfway between where you are in this vision, at the end of your career, and where you are today. Consider the following questions:

How are you stepping into your moxie? What people, projects, and passions are you giving your voice, time, energy, and resources to? How are you ensuring that you are on track to leave the legacy you were born to leave?

Time-travel backward again, this time to five years from today. Consider the exact same questions: How are you stepping into your moxie? What people, projects, and passions are you giving your voice, time, energy, and resources to? How are you ensuring that you are on track to leave the legacy you were born to leave?

Time-travel backward again, this time to one year from today. Consider the exact same questions: How are you stepping into your moxie? What people, projects, and passions are you giving your voice, time, energy, and resources to? How are you ensuring that you are on track to leave the legacy you were born to leave?

Time-travel backward, one last time, to three months from today. Consider the same questions: How are you stepping into your moxie? What people, projects, and passions are you giving your voice, time, energy, and resources to?

How are you ensuring that you apply your takeaways from this book to lay (or expand on) the foundation you must build to leave the legacy you were born to leave?

Now close your eyes and take a few minutes to recall what you saw for yourself ninety days, one year, and five years from now, midcareer, and at the end of your career. See how you have chosen thoughts and behaviors, created habits, and stepped into your moxie in both big and little ways to leave a powerful legacy.

QUESTIONS FOR REFLECTION

- What did you see for yourself in the Legacy Visualization? (Be sure to write it down.)
- What will you need to let go of (and conversely, what will you need to step into) to make your visualization a reality?
- Who are three people you can share your visualization discoveries with?
- After you finish the book, what will be your most immediate moxie-making action steps?

Over the past thirteen chapters I've provided you with stories, examples, and some occasional rabble-rousing to help you dial up your moxie, turn the volume way down on your self-doubt, and make each day a dress rehearsal for what you would say, and who you would be, if moxie was your default state. I challenge you to raise your hand for leadership opportunities. Chair meetings. Give speeches. Maybe even run for public office. Release attachment to the outcomes of what you say, and trust that when you (re)claim your voice and use it in a way that honors your beliefs and values, you will emancipate yourself from the agony of playing small, holding back, and speaking half-truths. And when your coworkers, colleagues, clients, family, and friends see you speaking out, sharing your ideas, challenging the status quo, and drawing attention to the people, projects, and passions that matter most to you, they will be receiving permission from you to do the same.

The legacy you saw yourself create was not an idle daydream, a possibility, something that could, maybe, one day happen. It's what you were put here to do and who you were put here to be. It's your responsibility to get out of your own way and bring it to fruition. Who you have been up until this point — whether you have been sheepish or brazen, jockeying for opportunities to shine or averting eye contact whenever someone throws your name into consideration for something that would elevate your visibility — choose to put your negative memories, diminishing behaviors, and self-sabotaging beliefs behind you. Your family, education, career, current W-2: they do not define you. Every day you get to write and speak the next chapter in the story you want to create.

When I withdrew from my first college, the week after I got back home I went to my first underage drinking party. I made more bad decisions in a twelve-hour period than most child stars make in a lifetime. I told my mom I was going to sleep over at a work friend's house, which was sort of true. Only rather than head over to my coworker Ashley's house, I went to another coworker, Iggy's. On the way, I rear-ended the car of another coworker, Ryan; told Ryan I might be gay when he professed his love to me later at the party; drank several beers (which is not so good when you have never had beer before and you're a teenager on an anti-depressant); and made out with Iggy's Ben Affleck–lookalike best friend most of the night, convinced that Ryan would understand once I explained everything to him the next morning. I made a bunch of other bad choices that night, like eating an entire apple pie à la mode and walking barefoot to and from the restaurant where I got said apple pie, but I think I've given you enough to appreciate the scope of my poor decision making.

When I woke up that next morning at Iggy's house, I knew I had effed up — and not just because my feet looked like they'd been barbecued, my mouth tasted like spoiled milk with a hint of Sour Patch Kids, and without my beer goggles Iggy's bestie (who had passed out on another couch) no longer bore the faintest resemblance to Ben Affleck. And yet I told myself, and believed every word, *Lex, you are not last night's semipsychotic behavior. You are a good person, built for greatness, and you will not throw away your potential or be so careless with another person's feelings ever again.*

I made good on my hungover vow. A few months later, I went back to college. And while my pathway to moxie in college and beyond, loooooooooong beyond, has not been straight, I never behaved that clumsily toward myself or another again. I believed and acted like I was someone who made things happen — and for the most part, I exceeded my own and others' expectations of me.

In my career, I've met CEOs who were teen moms. Community leaders who were once homeless. And more motivational speakers who were sexually abused, assaulted, or trafficked, in a few cases by their own families, than I care to count. Yet despite their environments or circumstances, these women, and in some instances men, chose moxie, even when it felt futile to do so. They chose to become protagonists in the story of their lives because the greatest payback is showing others who have held you back, especially yourself, *Imma be someone in this world.* What you choose to focus on is what you will create and make happen. Every idea you possess, every action you take, every dream you declare is possible for yourself — it is connected to your communication, to your inner, and in most instances your outer, voice.

So please, I implore you, make a pact with yourself that you will step into your moxie — regardless of how much back talk you hear in your head, or how much bile builds in your belly. For when you step into your moxie as if your life depends on it, because the quality of your life most certainly does, the sensation ultimately decreases and everything gets better, brighter, and easier. Now, the moxie path will inevitably have speed bumps. From time to time relationships and situations will get messy. Ryan, despite my repeated apologies, not too surprisingly never talked to me again. But long-term, when you choose moxie, you will experience more ease, more vitality, and deeper connection to yourself and others.

Can you imagine a world in which women and girls, regardless of nationality, race, class, age, gender identity, sexual orientation, or ability felt entitled to walk into any room, and onto any stage, and speak their truth? Imagine knowing, each and every day of *your* life, that what *you* say matters. Will elicit respect. Lead to action. Imagine asking for something when you wanted it. And when you didn't want something, saying no — and making it a complete sentence. Imagine when someone behaved badly, violated your boundaries, or abused his or her power, speaking up *and* forgiving them. Imagine staying out of judgment (of yourself and others), choosing impact over significance, as a result effecting meaningful, lasting change in the world.

Let's make this vision a reality together — one thought, one word, one sentence, one speech, one negotiation, one call to action at a time.

Mic drop.

Kidding, obviously.

Please, don't ever let your microphone go!

ACKNOWLEDGMENTS

Writing this book has been yummier than a golden chai latte, and for me that's really saying something. Truly, from the time I first sat my bum-bum down to write my book proposal through to typing out the closing remarks in my last chapter, birthing *Step into Your Moxie* has been one of my most joyful, intuitive, and purpose-filled professional endeavors I have ever experienced. I say this not to suggest that writing is easy, that the literary gods are sweet on me, or to elicit eye rolls or virtual backhands from anyone who has had a different relationship to writing. Rather, I feel compelled to acknowledge how grateful I am to no longer be circling around the perimeter of my purpose and to be able to write about, speak about, and coach in and from my passion zone. Thank you, precious reader, for reading my words, for letting them inspire your words, and for helping me leave my legacy by choosing to step into your moxie.

To my clients, particularly the women (and occasional men) in my Spotlight programs and in Influencer Academy — thank you for showing up for yourselves and for being such fabulous champions for one another. Thank you for trusting me as one of your guides and for reminding me each and every day that I step into my moxie so you have permission, and a pathway, to step into yours.

Big love to my agent, Steve Harris. Agent Steve, thank you for saying, "I want this book," for having an answer to all my questions (and I know, I ask a lot of questions), and for being a constant advocate for me and this work.

To the entire team at New World Library, I'm grateful to you for giving *Step into Your Moxie* a nurturing home to grow up in. Thank you, Marc Allen, for acquiring the book. Thank you, Georgia Hughes, my editor, for getting me and my point of view, and for the creative freedom to write the book I envisioned. Kristen Cashman, I thoroughly appreciate all your support in the homestretch with editing, design, and production. To my copyeditor, Mimi Kusch, thank you for letting me keep 90 percent of my humor and for cleaning up my grammar without taming my voice. And thank you, Kim Corbin, for working your marketing moxie to give this book an audience. A special thank-you also goes out to my New World Library sister from another mister, Corinne Zupko. Thank you for shepherding me through this process, for sharing your dos and don'ts, and for reminding me to breathe during the times when I forgot to.

What a dream come true to partner with the fine folks at Penguin Random House Audio on the audiobook for *Step into Your Moxie*. You all are true class acts. I appreciate your stellar recommendations for how to get ready, as well as your support during the recording process.

To the women in my Lady Authors Mastermind (yes, I'm sticking to our original name), thank you for inviting me into your coven when I was in the depths of PPD, for showing me that solopreneur-speaker-author-motherhood is messy for everyone, and for giving me permission to think outside the box about what this book would look like. For your feedback, advanced endorsements, and introductions, Halelly Azulay, Emily Bennington, Alexandra Levit, and Jodi Glickman, I am forever grateful.

To the women and men in The 108 and The Conquer Club, thank you for sharing one of the most important years of my life with me, for your inspiration, feedback, and courageous truth telling.

Victoriya Scovel, thank you for getting me through the homestretch of the writing and editing process, for laughing at all my jokes, and for always texting me right when I needed some of your boundless wisdom and cheerleading.

Jessica Tomlinson, thank you for believing in the Moxie Movement from the very beginning and for your friendship. You've been through *it all* with me — including that crazy laryngitis episode we'd both like to forget.

To my alma mater, Forest Ridge School of the Sacred Heart, thank you for instilling in me that I have a responsibility, as someone with tremendous privilege, to be a woman who can change the world. Class of 1998 — may we always know better, and with twenty years under our belts in the world, care enough to *do better*.

To my other teachers, mentors, and coaches, especially Jille Bartolome, Gabrielle Bernstein, Lori Lipman Brown, Kay Cannon, Jonathan Fields, Mitalene Fletcher, Nathalie Lussier, Natalie MacNeil, Cheryl Radeloff, Pamela Slim, Jon Stancato, Chris Vine, Renée West, and Helen White — whether you were in my life for a season or are hanging around for a lifetime, you each have shaped me as a speaker, author, coach, and thought leader in more ways than you will ever know.

Lots of consensual hugs and kisses go out to my business team, especially to Brittany Becher, Tressa Beheim, Stefanie

Frank, Lysa Greer, Cher Hale, Angela Stoner, Michael Vitone, Julie Waterhouse, and Stephenie Zamora. There is no way I could have had the bandwidth to write this book without you all working your magic behind the scenes, breathing life (and support) into the Moxie Movement.

To my family — Mom, Dad, Aunt Elaine, and Allen — thank you for your unconditional love and tireless championship. To my little Koukla, thank you for reinvigorating my purpose in this world, for unapologetically using your voice (even when Mommy tells you it's time to go to bed), and for bringing so much depth and meaning to my life.

And finally, to my partner in work and life, Stephen Oliveira — thank you for letting Lafitte bring you onstage, for wooing me with your homemade chocolate-covered strawberries, and for spending the past sixteen years illuminating what it looks like to be kind, compassionate, and committed to justice. There is nobody I would rather cocreate my future and watch *The Daily Show* with.

NOTES

Introduction

Page 2, *Media outlets such as CNN, PBS, and Inc.*: Marianne Schnall, "2018 Will Be the Year of Women," CNN, last modified December 15, 2017, https://www.cnn.com/2017/12/14/opinions/2018-will-be-the-year-of -women-schnall/index.html; Jessica Yarvin, "Will 2018 be the Next 'Year of the Woman'?" PBS News Hour, August 11, 2017, https://www.pbs.org /newshour/politics/will-2018-next-year-woman; James Kerr, "Will 2018 Be the Year of the Woman?" Inc., January 2, 2018, https://www.inc.com /james-kerr/will-2018-be-year-of-woman.html.

Page 3, *While the word didn't come into common use*: "Moxie," *Wikipedia*, last modified June 7, 2018, https://en.wikipedia.org/wiki/Moxie.

Page 6, *After a writer in the White House Office of Public Engagement*: Ronnie Cho, "Moxie Maven," President Barack Obama White House (blog), June 6, 2012, https://obamawhitehouse.archives.gov/blog/2012/06/06/moxie-maven.

Chapter 1. Headgear, Hairy Legs, and a Quarter Life of Humiliation

Page 11, *It takes years as a woman to unlearn*: Mercey Livingston, "5 Quotes to Live By from Amy Poehler's 'Yes Please,'" Mavenly + Co., March 29, 2017, https://mavenly.co/mavenly-co/5-quotes-live-by-poehlers-yes-please.

Chapter 2. Critics, Cops, and Cheerleaders...Oh My!

Page 32, *In her book* My Stroke of Insight: Jill Bolte Taylor, *My Stroke of Insight: A Brain Scientist's Personal Journey* (New York: Penguin, 2009), 120.

Chapter 3. Bunnies Don't Belong Here (but Cheetahs Do)

Page 44, *"The Dalai Lama says"*: Dalai Lama. "Nobel Laureates in Dialogue: Connecting for Peace" (panel, Vancouver Peace Summit, Vancouver, BC, September 27, 2009).

Chapter 4. Words, Words, Words

Page 55, *In Ives's world, Milton*: David Ives, "Words Words Words," in *All in the Timing* (New York: Dramatists Play Service, 1993).

Page 61, *In the 1984 movie*: The Karate Kid, directed by John G. Avildsen (1984; Los Angeles: Sony Pictures Home Entertainment, 2010), DVD.

Chapter 5. Your Gut as Your Guide

Page 71, *When you reach the end*: Kahlil Gibran, *Sand and Foam* (1926; repr., New York: Knopf, 1969), available at http://www-personal.umich.edu /~jrcole/gibran/sandfoam/sandfoam.htm.

Page 77, *At the time, I was reading*: Kerry Patterson, Joseph Grenny, Ron McMillan, and Al Switzler, *Crucial Conversations: Tools for Talking When Stakes Are High* (New York: McGraw-Hill, 2012), 11.

Chapter 6. Declare Your Desired Destination

Page 87, *If you don't know where you are going*: Forrest Gump, directed by Robert Zemeckis (1994; Los Angeles: Paramount Home Video, 2001), DVD.

Page 90, *Despite what Maria sings*: The Sound of Music, directed by Robert Wise (1965; Los Angeles: Twentieth Century Fox Home Entertainment, 2010), DVD.

Chapter 7. Go for the Holy Yes

Page 100, *But given that approximately 20 percent*: Linda Babcock and Sara Laschever, *Women Don't Ask: The High Cost of Avoiding Negotiation — and Positive Strategies for Change* (New York: Bantam, 2007), 11.

Page 102, *In the 1992 film*: David Mamet, *Glengarry Glen Ross*, directed by James Foley (1992; Los Angeles: Lionsgate Home Entertainment, 2002), DVD.

Page 102, *Chester Karrass, a renowned*: Dr. Chester Karrass's website, accessed December 27, 2017, https://www.karrass.com/dr-chester-karrass.

Page 104, *And by holy, I'm going*: Bible Hub HELPS Word-studies, "Hagios," accessed June 26, 2018, http://biblehub.com/greek/40.htm.

Page 108, *In their book* Yes!: Noah J. Goldstein, Steve J. Martin, and Robert B. Cialdini, *Yes! 50 Scientifically Proven Ways to Be Persuasive* (New York: Free Press, 2008), 150–54.

Page 110, *You likely have encountered the Chinese word*: Merriam-Webster.com, s.v. "chi," accessed December 27, 2017, https://www.merriam-webster.com/dictionary/chi.

Chapter 8. Your Spotlight Is Waiting

Page 123, *And while popular psychology*: James Clear, "How Long Does It Actually Take to Form a New Habit? (Backed by Science)," *Huffington Post*, May 29, 2015, last modified May 29, 2016, https://www.huffingtonpost.com/james-clear/form-new-habits_b_7346170.html.

Page 124, *As I shared in chapter 2*: Jill Bolte Taylor, *My Stroke of Insight: A Brain Scientist's Personal Journey* (New York: Penguin, 2009), 120.

Page 129, *As self-help pioneer Louise Hay*: Robert Holden, "What Is Mirror Work: An Introduction to Louise Hay's Famous Exercise" (blog), accessed December 27, 2017, https://www.robertholden.org/blog/what-is-mirror-work.

Chapter 9. What to Say When the Spotlight Is Yours

Page 133, *We love seeing raw truth*: Brené Brown, *Daring Greatly: How the Courage to Be Vulnerable Transforms the Way We Live, Love, Parent, and Lead* (New York: Avery, 2015), 41.

Page 133, *When I read Shonda Rhimes's memoir*: Shonda Rhimes, *Year of Yes: How to Dance It Out, Stand in the Sun, and Be Your Own Person* (New York: Simon & Schuster, 2015), xiii–xxiii.

Chapter 10. Conflict Is the Pits, Until It Isn't

Page 164, *According to the Childhood*: "You Are Not Alone," Childhood Domestic Violence Association, "10 Startling Statistics about Children of Domestic Violence," February 21, 2014, https://cdv.org/2014/02/10-startling-domestic-violence-statistics-for-children.

Page 164, *According to the US Department*: "How Common Is PTSD," US Department of Veteran Affairs, accessed December 27, 2017, https://www.ptsd .va.gov/public/PTSD-overview/basics/how-common-is-ptsd.asp.

Chapter 11. Susan B. Anthony Didn't Fight for Your Right to Be a Meanie

Page 167, *An abolitionist, educational reformer*: National Susan B. Anthony Museum & House, accessed December 27, 2017, http://susanbanthony house.org/index.php.

Page 170, *A 2016 national survey*: Weiyi Cai and Scott Clement, "What Americans Think about Feminism Today," *Washington Post*, January 27, 2016, https://www.washingtonpost.com/graphics/national/feminism-project/poll.

Page 182, *Nary a week goes by*: Tracy Chapman, "Fast Car" (New York: Elektra, 1988), https://genius.com/Tracy-chapman-fast-car-official-lyrics.

Chapter 12. When the Universe Bites Your Bum-Bum, Don't Let Her Steal Your Voice

Page 185, *You may write me down in history*: Maya Angelou, "And Still I Rise," from *And Still I Rise* (New York: Random House, 1978), 41.

Page 190, *Oprah Winfrey, for example*: "Oprah Winfrey," *Wikipedia*, last modified June 14, 2018, accessed December 27, 2017, https://en.wikipedia.org /wiki/Oprah_Winfrey.

Page 190, *J. K. Rowling was a depressed*: "J. K. Rowling," *Wikipedia*, last modified June 10, 2018, accessed December 27, 2017, https://en.wikipedia.org /wiki/J._K._Rowling.

Page 190, *And one of my favorite*: Vishrut Shah, "Elon Musk and the Art of Failing Successfully," YourStory, June 28, 2016, accessed December 30, 2017, https://yourstory.com/2016/06/elon-musk-failure.

Page 198, Resilience *is defined both as*: En.OxfordDictionaries.com, s.v. "resilience," accessed December 27, 2017, https://en.oxforddictionaries.com /definition/resilience.

Chapter 13. Choose Legacy Over Fame

Page 209, *In a* New York Times *interview*: Sandra Garcia, "The Woman Who Created #MeToo Long Before Hashtags," *New York Times*, October 20, 2017,

https://www.nytimes.com/2017/10/20/us/me-too-movement-tarana
-burke.html.

Page 210, *Diane Simone is another example*: Bud Kennedy, "20 Years, 794
Rescues: How a Hood County Woman Thought up Amber Alerts," *Star-
Telegram*, January 14, 2016, http://www.star-telegram.com/opinion/opn
-columns-blogs/bud-kennedy/article54808010.html.

Page 210, *And over the past twenty years*: Diana Simone, "Amber Alert: The
Power of Response-Ability" (TEDx Talk, Wilmington, DE, November 2,
2017), https://www.youtube.com/watch?v=8gSIQr2YzMg.

INDEX

action. *See* calls to action
adjectives/adverbs, overuse of, 60–61
aha moments, 142
AlexiaVernon.com, 9, 37, 50, 83, 131, 164, 211
Alien (film; 1979), 44
"Always Be Closing" (masculine negotiation style), 102, 103, 104–5, 110
AMBER Alerts, 210
Angelou, Maya, 185
anger: author's experiences, 169–70; determining levels of, 171–72; feminist movement and, 170–71
Anthony, Susan B., 167–68, 176, 182
anxiety, 23–24
apologies, 43
attacks, personal, 152
audience: storytelling to ignite discovery in, 138–43; time-sensitivity and benefits for, 109, 111–12; visibility fears before, 117–21; visualizing, 98
avoidance, 150

Babcock, Linda, 101
backsliding, 8
Balanchine, George, 80
Baldwin, Alec, 102
"because" statements, 108
Before You Ask, Listen (Moxie Moment exercise), 114–15
belief, permission for, 97–98
best-case scenarios, 24
Beyoncé (actress/singer), 41, 136
black-and-white thinking, 28–30
blaming, 157, 161–62
"bless and release," 153

blog posts, 207

bodily sensation: daring conversations and, 153; feelings experienced as, 124–25; reverse-engineering and, 93; visibility fears as, 121–23, 136

body language, 45, 47–48, 122, 154–55

body shaming, 15

boundaries, articulating, 8; author's experiences, 174–75, 177–78; benefits of, 173–74; clarity about, 181–82; essentials of, 177–79; moxie amplified by, 164–65, 175–76, 181–83; Moxie Moment exercise, 179–81; need for, 172–73; women and, 173

breathing, 110, 125, 155

Brown, Brené, 133

Buff Up Your Capacity for Visibility (Moxie Moment exercise), 128–32

bullying behavior, 161

bum-bum-biting moments. *See* setbacks

bunnyitis: author's experiences, 41–43; boundary setting and, 173; characteristics of, 43–44, 45–46, 47; negotiation and, 103, 107; recommendations for, 52; word choices for curing, 59–64

Burke, Tarana, 209–10

"but" statements, 62, 158

calls to action: failure to make, 44; follow-through on, 45; persuasion as leader to, 96; reverse-engineering from, 90–93, 94–95, 141–42; storytelling and, 141–43

Carter, Majora, 205

Chapman, Tracy, 168, 182

checking out, 160

Cheerleader, inner, 30–31, 33, 36, 38

Cheetah, inner, 46–49, 52–53

chi, using, 110

Childhood Domestic Violence Association, 164

Cialdini, Robert, 108

classism, 3, 6

Clear the Voice of Fear and Let Your Intuition Speak (Moxie Moment exercise), 83–85

client communication, 180–81

clothing choices, 59

CNN, 2

Coach, inner, 31–32, 34–36, 38–39, 46

cognitive intuition, 79

Come to Jesus moments, 19–21, 138, 139

communication: as habit based, 123; intuition as guide for, 74–76; presence for, 131–32. *See also* communication styles

Communication Audit (Moxie Moment exercise), 49–54

communication styles: author's experiences, 41–43; cheetah-like, 46–49, 53–54; masculine vs. feminine, 5–6; Moxie Moment exercise, 49–54; personal stories about, 17–19; tone-deafness to, 57–58. *See also* bunnyitis; dragonosis

community, creating, 106

confidence, women's lack of, 1–3

conflict, 145; author's experiences,

147–49; causes of/solutions to, 159–63; "little-*c* vs. Capital-*C*," 164; Moxie Moment exercise, 163–64; self-created, 149–51; word choices and, 155–56. *See also* daring conversations

conversations: difficult, 150–51, 157–58; necessary, 150; speaking truth in, 207. *See also* daring conversations

Cop, inner, 28–30, 33, 35–36, 38

cosmic winks, 8, 189–90

Crawford, Joan, 44

creativity, 199

Critic, inner, 26–28, 33, 35, 37–38, 140

Crucial Conversations (Patterson et al.), 77

Dalai Lama, 44

dance, 129–30

Dance the Demons Out (exercise), 129–30

daring conversations: cocreating, 153–55; difficult conversations turned into, 150–51; preparing for, 151–53; successful, 155; word choices during, 152–53, 155–58

defensiveness, 162–63

Devil Wears Prada, The (film; 2006), 44

difficult behavior, causes/solutions, 159–63

disclaimers, 61–62

divine, the, 195

domestic violence, 164

dragonosis: boundary setting and, 173–74; characteristics of, 44–45,

47, 64–65; negotiation and, 103; recommendations for, 52–53; word choices for curing, 65–66

Dyer, Wayne, 147

electronic devices, turning off, 177–78

emails, 172, 178

emotions, 45, 47, 124–25, 153

empathy, 199

endorphins, 130

entertainment, 94, 139–40

experiential intuition, 79

eye contact, 45, 47

fame, 207, 209

fears, 23–24, 138. *See also* visibility fears

feedback, 45; intuition and, 80–83; masculine vs. feminine styles, 208

feminine power spectrum, 43, 44

feminism, 168–71

filler words, 67–68, 126

financial freedom, 177, 178

Five Rs, The (Moxie Moment exercise), 20–21

flexibility, 45, 47

forgiveness, 137, 153, 159

Forrest Gump (film; 1994), 87

Friedan, Betty, 168

Gay-Straight Student Alliance, 169

gender bias, 6, 169, 171

gender nonbinary people, 7

Gibran, Kahlil, 71

gifts, personalized, 105

Glengarry Glen Ross (film; 1992), 102

God, 193, 194, 195, 196
"Go for the Holy Yes" (feminine
    negotiation style), 104–5. *See also*
    holy selling
Goldstein, Noah, 108
gossiping, 158
gratitude, 124–25, 128–29, 156
Gratitude Mirror Work (exercise),
    128–29

habits, 34, 123
Hagerman, Amber, 210
Harry Potter and the Sorcerer's Stone
    (Rowling), 190
Hathaway, Anne, 194
Hey, Boundary! (Moxie Moment
    exercise), 179–81
hiding out, 159–60
Hollywood voiceover strategy, 194, 195
holy selling: author's experiences,
    111–14; characteristics of, 105–10;
    masculine negotiation style vs.,
    104–5; Moxie Moment exercise,
    114–15; "not yes yet" moments and,
    101–2, 111–14
homophobia, 169
"hopefully" statements, 61
humor, 47

Ice, Auliq, 55
idea-bashing, 64–66
"I'm fine" statements, 66
"I'm sorry" statements, 63–64, 156–57
*In Business as in Life — You Don't Get
    What You Deserve, You Get What
    You Negotiate* (Karrass), 103

Inc., 2
indigestion, 73–74
inflexibility, 45
influence: as act of service, 8–9,
    164–65; amplifying, 4, 7; commu-
    nication styles and, 43, 45, 52–53;
    entertainment vs., 94; female,
    media portrayals of, 45; holy
    selling and, 104, 106; lack of, 44;
    masculine vs. feminine models, 5;
    reverse-engineering and, 93–94;
    self-connection and, 54; through
    storytelling, 139; use of, in leader-
    ship, 176, 206–7, 210; verbosity
    vs., 63; word choices and, 60–61,
    66–67
insecurity, 1–3
insufficiency, fear of, 126
intuition, 7; author's experiences,
    71–74, 80–81; boundary setting
    and, 177; calling in, for communi-
    cation, 74–76; defined, 73–74; feed-
    back filtered through, 80–83; how
    it works, 76–79; Moxie Moment
    exercise, 83–85; reason vs., 75;
    recognizing, 78–79; types of, 79
"I think," "I feel," "I believe," "I mean"
    statements, 60
Ives, David, 55–56

Kaiser Family Foundation, 170–71
Karate Kid, The (film; 1984), 61
Karrass, Chester, 102–3
Kenworthy, Gus, 117
kinesthetic intuition, 79
Knowles, Beyoncé, 41, 136

Laschever, Sara, 101
leadership: author as coach of, 1, 6, 44, 48–49, 76, 113, 170, 188; boundary setting and, 175–76; meaning of, 209; setbacks as opportunities for, 165, 190; thought leadership, 197, 202; women in, 208, 209–10
leadership skills, 175–76
legacy, 202–3; author's experiences, 205–7, 214–16; creating one's own, 210–11, 213–14; Moxie Moment exercises, 211–13; speaking truth as, 207–11
Legacy Visualization (Moxie Moment exercise), 211–13
Let Your Story Transform the Lives of Others (Moxie Moment exercise), 202
listening, 154–55
Little Mermaid, The (film; 1989), 188–89
loved ones, quality time with/away from, 177, 178
Love Up on Your Difficult People (Moxie Moment exercise), 163–64

Mamet, David, 102
Martin, Steve J., 108
"maybe" statements, 61
media interviews, 207
memorizing, 122
men, 7, 170, 208
mental scripting, 150
#MeToo movement, 209–10
mic, sharing, 208–9
mirroring, 107, 128–29

Miss Junior America Pageant, 2, 16, 46
misunderstandings, identifying, 155
motivation, 25
moxie: amplifying, 172–76; author's development of, 4–6, 133–36, 215–16; boundary articulation for staying in, 164–65, 175–76, 181–83; communication styles and, 54; cultivation of, 115; defined, 3–4, 54; hijacking of, 171–72; hurdles to, 102; influence of, 8–9; legacy and, 202–3, 210–11; as lifelong habit, 22–24; self-talk and, 32–36; setbacks and, 192, 198–201; stepping into, 8, 36, 37, 40, 64, 115, 121, 177, 192, 198, 210–11; stepping out of, 46, 100; stories as birthplace of, 16–19; tenets of, 119–20, 208–9
Moxie Moment exercises: boundary setting, 179–81; communication styles, 49–54; conflict, 163–64; holy selling, 114–15; how to use, 9, 19–20; intuition, 83–85; legacy, 211–13; reverse-engineering, 96–98; self-talk, 37–39; setbacks, 202; stories/storytelling, 20–21, 143–45; visibility fears, 128–32; word choices, 67–69
Moxie Nerve Food, 3–4
Musk, Elon, 190–91
My Stroke of Insight (Taylor), 32

name-calling, 65–66
National American Woman Suffrage Association, 167

National Organization for Women
    (NOW), 169
negotiation: author's experiences,
    100–102; masculine vs. femi-
    nine styles, 102, 103–5; women's
    avoidance of, 101, 103. *See also* holy
    selling
nervousness, 41
New York Times, 209
Nineteenth Amendment, 168
nonverbal communication, 154–55
"not yes yet" moments, 101–2, 111–14

objections, potential, 106–7
overexplanations, 44

passive-aggressive behavior, 66
payoff, demonstrating, 107–8
PBS, 2
persuasion: author's experiences,
    99–102; calls to action and, 96;
    story-based, 109–10. *See also* holy
    selling; negotiation
Phelps, Fred, Sr., 169
plagiarism, 68–69
pleasure, focus on, 108–9
Poehler, Amy, 11
points of view: other, 154; uncompel-
    ling, 44
post-partum depression (PPD),
    186–88, 195, 196
Power Up Your Inner Coach (Moxie
    Moment exercise), 37–39
presence, 20, 40, 47, 131–32, 177
"probably" statements, 61
PTSD, 164

public speaking, 12–13, 48, 118, 123, 138
purpose, 20

qualifying phrases/statements, 61–62
questions: angry rhetorical, 66;
    approval-seeking, 63; Coach
    questions, 34–36, 38–39, 46; during
    daring conversations, 152; payoff
    demonstrated through, 107–8

racism, 3, 6, 169
reapplying, 21
reason, 75, 109–10
recalling, 20
reframing, 20–21
rehearsing, 123, 126
releasing, 21
reliving, 20
resilience: author's experiences,
    191–98; benefits of, 198–201; celeb-
    rity examples, 190–91; defined, 198;
    strategies for, 194–95, 197
resources, 9
reverse-engineering: author's experi-
    ences, 87–90; call to action as
    starting point of, 90–93, 94–95,
    141–42; of daring conversations,
    152; Moxie Moment exercise,
    96–98; for speeches/presentations,
    93–96
Reverse-Engineer Your Communi-
    cation (Moxie Moment exercise),
    96–98
Rhimes, Shonda, 45, 133
role-playing, 113, 122, 150
Rowling, J. K., 190

Sandberg, Sheryl, 113–14
scheduling, 178
self-awareness, 201
self-connection, 54
self-esteem, 6
self-perception, 17
self-reproach, 158, 195
Self-Service Visualization (exercise),
    130–31
self-talk: addressing, 22; author's
    experiences, 25–26, 136; Coach
    intervention in, 34–39; conflict
    and, 149; empowering, 195; inabil-
    ity to stop, 1–3; inner voices influ-
    encing, 26–32; moxie influenced
    by, 32–36; Moxie Moment exercise,
    37–39; negative, 76, 149; self-
    empowering choices in, 7; stories
    triggering, 17–19
service, acts of, 8, 9–10, 207–11, 216
setbacks: author's experiences, 185–88;
    as cosmic winks, 189–90; as gifts,
    198–201; Moxie Moment exercise,
    202; resilience and recalibration
    from, 190–98
sexism, 3, 6, 169
sexual abuse, 209–10
Simone, Diana, 210
sleep, 177–78
smiling, 47, 49, 67–69, 126
socialization process, 171
social media, 172
"sorry" statements, 63–64, 156–57
Space Academy, 14–16
speeches/presentations: author's
    experiences, 135, 136; fears while

giving, 117–21, 136; rehearsing, 123,
    126; reverse-engineering for, 93–96;
    storytelling during, 138–43
stance, 47–48
Stanton, Elizabeth Cady, 167–68
Steinem, Gloria, 168
Stop and Smile (Moxie Moment
    exercise), 67–69, 126
stories: Come to Jesus, 19–21, 138,
    139; about communication styles,
    17–19; everyday, 140; hiding in,
    136; internal self-defeating, 11–16;
    as moxie birthplace, 16–19; Moxie
    Moment exercises, 20–21, 143–45;
    persuasion based on, 109–10;
    rewriting, 22–24; self-talk and, 22;
    sharing, 137–38, 154
storytelling, 47; author's experiences,
    136–38; discovery ignited in audi-
    ence by, 138–43; Moxie Moment
    exercise, 143–45
Streep, Meryl, 44
success, 194–95, 198
succinctness, 63
support, receiving, 200–201

Taylor, Jill Bolte, 32, 33, 124
TED Talks, 136, 140, 210
"Tell me more" statements, 156
Tesla, 190–91
"thank you," 156
"That's not my problem/responsibil-
    ity" statements, 158
"That's not what I..." statements,
    157–58
Thompson, Augustin, 3–4

Thoreau, Henry David, 99
thought leadership, 197, 202
time, perceptions of, 177, 178
time-sensitivity, 109, 111–12
tone-deafness, 57–58
transgender people, 7
transparency, 200
triangulation, 158
Truth, Sojourner, 168
truth(s): feedback and, 82–83; shar-
    ing, during daring conversations,
    152, 155, 156
truth telling: as act of service, 8, 9–10,
    207–11, 216; author's experiences,
    132–38; as feminine influence
    model, 5; gratitude for, during
    daring conversations, 156; holy
    selling and, 104, 106; legacy and, 10;
    moxie required for, 2; parameters
    for, 136–38; visibility fears and, 52,
    121; worst-case scenarios, 23–24
trying vs. doing, 61

United States Department of Veterans
    Affairs, 164
universe, the, 195, 196
Use a Story to Facilitate an Aha
    (Moxie Moment exercise), 143–45

verbosity, 63
verbs, weak, overuse of, 61
violent phraseology, 66–67
visibility: amplifying, 4, 8, 214;
    author's desire for, 206; claiming,
    9–10, 118; increasing capacity for
    (Moxie Moment exercise), 128–32;

legacy and elevation of, 214;
    opportunities for, 84–85
visibility fears: author's experi-
    ences, 11–16, 117–21, 136, 207;
    Moxie Moment exercises, 128–32;
    playing nicely with, 124–28, 145;
    reverse-engineering and, 93; as
    sensation, 121–23, 136; worst-case
    scenarios, 16, 24
voice, 20; amplifying, 4; finding,
    39–40, 69; pitching up of, 62–63;
    tone of, 154–55
voices, inner: Cheerleader, 30–31, 33,
    36, 38; Coach, 31–32, 34–36, 38–39,
    46; Cop, 28–30, 33, 35–36, 38; Critic,
    26–28, 33, 34, 37–38

Washington Post, 170–71
Weaver, Sigourney, 44
"we" statements, 157
"What I want for us is…," 156
"When I Look at You, I See…"
    (exercise), 128
White House Office of Public
    Engagement, 6
Winfrey, Oprah, 153, 190
winging, 150, 151
woman's suffrage, 167–68
women: angry, 170–71; boundary-set-
    ting needs of, 173, 176; in leader-
    ship roles, 208, 209–10; negotiation
    avoided by, 101, 103; truth telling
    by, 216; vocal pitching up of, 62–63
Women Don't Ask (Babcock and
    Laschever), 101
women's leadership programs, 48–49

word choices: author's experiences,
58–59, 64–65; community created
through, 106; for curing bunnyitis, 59–64; for curing dragonosis,
65–67; during daring conversations, 152–53, 155–58; filler words,
67–68, 126; Moxie Moment exercise, 67–69
Words, Words, Words (drama; Ives),
55–56
Working Girl (film; 1988), 44

workplace, speaking truth at, 207
worst-case scenarios, 23–24

"year of the woman," 2
Year of Yes (Rhimes), 133
yelling, 161
"yes": as birthright, 110; during daring
conversations, 156
"you" statements, 157

Ziglar, Zig, 25

ABOUT THE AUTHOR

Branded a "Moxie Maven" by President Obama's White House Office of Public Engagement for her unique and effective approach to women's empowerment, Alexia Vernon is a sought-after speaking coach to female (and male) executives, media personalities, entrepreneurs, business professionals, and change-makers who want to spread their ideas, positively impact people's lives, and advance their thought leadership. Alexia is the creator of the Spotlight speaking community, and she has supported thousands of speakers through her online trainings, live events, the Spotlight Speaker Accelerator coaching program, and her premier mastermind, the Spotlight Speakers Collective.

Alexia has delivered transformational keynotes and corporate trainings for Fortune 500 companies, college campuses, professional associations, and the United Nations, and she is also a TEDxWomen speaker. Alexia has gotten her gab on with media such as CNN, NBC, ABC, CBS, Forbes.com, Inc.com, the *European Business Review*, and *Women's Health* magazine.

Alexia lives in Las Vegas, Nevada, with her partner in business and life, Stephen, and their precocious, wide-eyed daughter. Connect with Alexia online at AlexiaVernon.com. For work-sheets, meditations, and other supplemental materials related to the book, visit AlexiaVernon.com/MoxieBook.

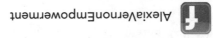 AlexiaVernonEmpowerment

 Alexia Vernon

 @AlexiaVernon

NEW WORLD LIBRARY is dedicated to publishing books and other media that inspire and challenge us to improve the quality of our lives and the world. We are a socially and environmentally aware company. We recognize that we have an ethical responsibility to our customers, our staff members, and our planet.

We serve our customers by creating the finest publications possible on personal growth, creativity, spirituality, wellness, and other areas of emerging importance. We serve New World Library employees with generous benefits, significant profit sharing, and constant encouragement to pursue their most expansive dreams.

As a member of the Green Press Initiative, we print an increasing number of books with soy-based ink on 100 percent postconsumer-waste recycled paper. Also, we power our offices with solar energy and contribute to nonprofit organizations working to make the world a better place for us all.

Our products are available in bookstores everywhere.

www.newworldlibrary.com

At NewWorldLibrary.com you can download our catalog,
subscribe to our e-newsletter, read our blog,
and link to authors' websites, videos, and podcasts.

Find us on Facebook, follow us on Twitter, and watch us on YouTube.

Send your questions and comments our way!
You make it possible for us to do what we love to do.

Phone: 415-884-2100 or 800-972-6657
Catalog requests: Ext. 10 | Orders: Ext. 10 | Fax: 415-884-2199
escort@newworldlibrary.com

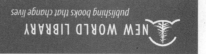

NEW WORLD LIBRARY

publishing books that change lives   14 Pamaron Way, Novato, CA 94949